TACK AND CLOTHING

WARD LOCK RIDING SCHOOL

KNOW YOUR PONY
UNDERSTANDING YOUR HORSE
LEARNING TO RIDE
DISCOVERING DRESSAGE
EVENTING
UNDERSTANDING FITNESS AND TRAINING
PRACTICAL SHOWJUMPING
MODERN STABLE MANAGEMENT

TACK AND CLOTHING

SUSAN McBANE

WARD LOCK

RIDING SCHOOL

WARD LOCK

This book is dedicated to
RA,
a dog and a half

A WARD LOCK BOOK

First published in the UK 1993
by Ward Lock
Villiers House 41/47 Strand
London WC2N 5JE

A Cassell Imprint

Distributed in the United States
by Sterling Publishing Co., Inc.
387 Park Avenue South, New York, NY 10016-8810

Distributed in Australia
by Capricorn Link (Australia) Pty Ltd
P.O. Box 665, Lane Cove, NSW 2066

A British Library Cataloguing in Publication Data Block for
this book may be obtained from the British Library.

ISBN 0 7063 7145 3

All photographs by Kit Houghton

Printed and bound in Great Britain by Hillman Printers (Frome) Ltd

Frontispiece: Checking the fit of a standing martingale

CONTENTS

THE AUTHOR

Susan McBane began riding at the age of four and has had many years experience of riding and looking after her own and other people's horses and ponies, in widely differing circumstances.

She has been a specialist equestrian writer for 23 years and her work appears regularly in most major equestrian magazines in the United Kingdom, with some overseas contributions. She has 14 books in print.

In 1980 she founded EQUI magazine and edited this highly respected journal until, under new ownership, it ceased publication in 1985. She also helped found the Equine Behaviour Study Circle in 1978 and is still Editor-in-Chief of its newsletter, *Equine Behaviour*.

She has an interest in the life sciences and is noted for bringing sound scientific fact to her writing, while presenting it in an easy-to-read and easily understood style. She has been described as one of Britain's leading equestrian writers, always emphasizing the practical aspects and effective principles of horse and pony management.

CHAPTER 1

A FEW
PRELIMINARIES

It is very easy to spend more on your horse's tack, clothing and other general equipment than on the price of the horse himself! The range of items for you to choose from nowadays is extensive and the design and purpose of some items may confuse even experienced horse people. No wonder the less experienced can become not only bewildered but also worried. 'What exactly do I need?' they may think. 'Do I really have to own *all* of this? What is everything for; how do I use it – and how much will it all cost?'

Relax! Would it comfort you to know that you require only a tiny fraction of the gear confronting you in any decent tack shop? In practice, you can look after a horse, ride him and keep him warm and well cared for with surprisingly little equipment, provided you get the right things to start with. You can begin with a simple range of items and add on as much or as little as you feel you need, or want, later on.

ESSENTIALS

So what do you really need in the way of tack, clothing and other equipment when you own a horse or pony that is in work, as opposed to retired or used only for breeding?

If you wish to ride in reasonable comfort you will need a saddle although it is quite possible to ride in a safe, enclosed area on a blanket kept on by means of a roller or surcingle. Obviously, you will not have any stirrups riding this way, but years ago this was a favoured way of giving novices a really close feel of their mount and his movement underneath them. Assuming, however, that you do wish to use a saddle, probably the most useful sort to buy, which will see you through all types of riding, is a general purpose, event or cross-country saddle; this is shaped so that whether you use a longish stirrup-leather length for flatwork (non-jumping) or a shorter one for either show jumping or cross-country jumping, your knees will fit into the saddle flap and your legs will be secure and comfortable. Your seat will also be accommodated correctly whatever position you adopt. You will also need a girth to keep your saddle on, a pair of stirrups and a pair of stirrup leathers.

It is possible to ride in an enclosed area in just a headcollar with a rope to your hand but this is not very safe! A bridle of some sort is really essential, together with a bit unless you want a bitless bridle (which can be very effective on some horses) and a pair of reins (or two pairs depending on your bitting arrangement). Other tack you may see on riding horses, such as martingales, neck-straps, cruppers (rare), boots and bandages are not essential unless your horse's conformation or action makes them appropriate.

Lungeing equipment, such as a cavesson, roller, breastgirth, crupper, side reins, boots, lungeing whip and rein, is only needed if you are going to lunge your horse. It is sometimes useful to be able to do this but it is by no means essential.

Clothing

What about clothing? Again, you could manage with none at all if your horse is a toughish sort and is going to keep his natural coat at all times or be only very lightly clipped. Summer clothing (usually cotton or linen summer sheets) may be used to keep the coat of a groomed, stabled horse free from stable dust and debris and may be regarded as essential in a showing yard, but is not necessary for 'ordinary' horses or ponies. If you are going to clip and work your horse in winter, you will need two stable rugs, so that you can use one while the other is being laundered. You must replace the coat you remove to keep the horse warm. If your horse is very fine-skinned and you remove most of his coat, you may also need blankets or under-rugs. If he is going to be turned out at all in winter, he will need a waterproof turnout rug if he is clipped or thin-skinned and fine-coated. British winters are too harsh

for such horses to be turned out without protection. Cold, wet and windy weather creates ideal conditions for the development of severe chills or even hypothermia, even if the horse is well fed and in good condition.

If you have only one indoor rug (normally called stable rug these days rather than the more precise, traditional terms of day rug and night rug, as modern synthetic fabrics have made the differentiation between the two obsolete) and only one outdoor, turnout rug, you could manage with just these if you use the turnout rug on the horse while his stable rug is being washed. However, this becomes more difficult if the rug is covered in wet mud and, obviously, you can't turn him out in his stable rug. Normally, life is easier if you have two stable rugs and two turnout rugs so that they can all be used and cared for properly. However, with modern synthetic turnout rugs it is quite possible to wash and dry them overnight – into the washing machine at teatime, provided your machine is big enough, when he comes in and back on the horse next morning when he goes out for the day – so you could manage with only one of these, and they *can* be expensive. Relax again. You don't have to wash them every day or even every week. Often just letting them dry overnight and probably picking off the mud next morning is sufficient.

You will also need a headcollar and leadrope to lead your horse in and out from the field and for tying him up when necessary. It is not really practical to lead with a bridle every time (although this is highly desirable if you are leading on a road)

From top left clockwise: waterproof turnout rug of good, modern design; snaffle bridle; well-designed and shaped modern stable rug; general purpose saddle with girth, stirrups and stirrup leathers.

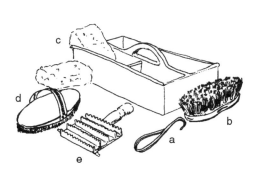

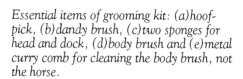

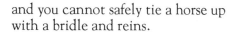

Essential items of grooming kit: (a)hoof-pick, (b)dandy brush, (c)two sponges for head and dock, (d)body brush and (e)metal curry comb for cleaning the body brush, not the horse.

A full haynet, two water buckets and a squatter feeding bucket.

and you cannot safely tie a horse up with a bridle and reins.

Stable equipment

You will need a very basic grooming kit – hoofpick, dandy brush and sponges for his head and dock. If you want to groom your horse properly and keep him really clean, you will certainly need a body brush and curry comb. You would find a rubber and/or plastic curry comb useful for removing dried mud and stable stains (dried-on urine and droppings). A water brush is not essential but is useful for 'laying' (damping) the mane and tail to smooth them down. Other grooming items are not essential.

You will need containers to hold water in the stable – usually a couple of buckets (one does not hold enough for a horse stabled overnight or while his owner is at work all day), a small plastic dustbin or, if your stables are so equipped, an automatic waterer.

You could actually get away with feeding your horse on a clean piece of sheeting or sacking placed on the floor in the stable, but a wide bucket, washing-up bowl or proper manger would be more useful, especially if the horse is not a tidy feeder. In any case, you have to carry the feed to the horse in something so you might as well get a feed bucket.

You can feed hay loose in a *clean* corner as is common practice on many top studs, or you may prefer to use a haynet or hayrack.

If you keep your horse at livery, mucking-out tools will probably be provided, otherwise you will need a shovel and a fork for whatever type of bedding you are using. You will also need some means of carrying the muck to the manure heap – either a wheelbarrow or a muck sack, usually made of something like polypropylene with a drawstring round the edge that can be pulled closed when you have enough muck on the sack. Few women and girls use these, though, as they are extremely heavy when full, so a wheelbarrow might

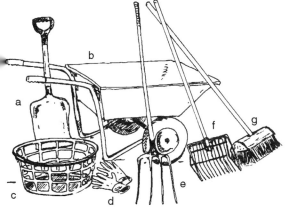

Mucking out tools and tack-cleaning kit:
(a) droppings shovel, (b) two-wheeled
barrow (more stable than single-wheel),
(c) muck skep, (d) rubber gloves, (e) four-
tined fork for straw, (f) shavings rake,
(g) broom, (h) bucket, (i) thin soaping
sponge, (j) chamois leather, (k) metal polish
(you will also need a rag and duster),
(l) saddle soap, (m) washing sponge.

well be needed. You will also need a
yard broom to keep the yard tidy.

To clean your tack, if it is made of
leather, as most still is these days,
you will need two sponges, perhaps
a chamois leather or synthetic
equivalent, a bucket for water, saddle
soap and metal polish. Textiles like
numnahs and rugs can be washed
with ordinary non-biological washing products, and treated with fabric
softener as a beneficial bonus in the
last rinse. Leather dressing is not
essential for tack that is regularly
cleaned with glycerine saddle soap.
A stable rubber, of the kind used to
finish off a body-brushed horse, is
also useful for drying and polishing
metal items like stirrups and bits.
You will also need two rags or
dusters for applying the metal polish
to the tack.

Essential basic tack
U saddle with stirrups, leathers and girth
bridle

Essential basic clothing
U 1 or 2 stable rugs
U 1 or 2 blankets or under-rugs
U 1 or 2 turnout rugs
U headcollar and leadrope

Essential basic stable equipment
Essential grooming kit
U hoofpick
U dandy brush
U 2 sponges

Desirable extras
U metal curry comb
U plastic curry comb
U water brush
U body brush

Yard kit
U 2 water buckets or 1 small plastic
U dustbin
U feed bowl
U haynet
U shovel
U fork
U wheelbarrow or muck sack
U yard broom

Basic tack-cleaning equipment
U 2 sponges
U chamois leather or similar
U bucket
U saddle soap
U metal polish plus rags and duster
U stable rubber

And that, really, is it. The more you have to do with horses, the more you will discover about what kit is available and you may well add to your equipment as you go along, but the list on page 11 comprises the basic essentials that will make life with a working horse possible and easy. Anything else may be regarded as a bonus.

QUALITY, TYPE AND FIT

It is important to buy good-quality tack as poor-quality equipment can actually be dangerous. It is far better to buy second-hand, good tack than poor-quality new. If you are inexperienced, it helps to take an experienced friend or advisor with you when shopping. In any case, it is safest always to shop at a retail outlet that is a member of the Society of Master Saddlers and/or the British Equestrian Trade Association. If you look for one or both of these signs, you should be assured of not only good-quality equipment but also expert, reliable advice and help with your requirements.

Such saddlers or retailers often have a good selection of second-hand equipment that has many years of life left in it. It will usually have been fully overhauled and repaired before going on sale and you should be able to buy it with confidence.

If you feel you need advice from a professional horse person, seek out a qualified instructor or other professional with British Horse Society or Association of British Riding Schools qualifications. Both these bodies run stringent examination structures and people with these qualifications will know enough about tack to ensure that you buy suitable equipment for your needs.

Most of the best tack on sale in the UK is British or European. Very little American tack is sold in the UK and most of the European tack available here (other than British) is German. When examining any equipment, check the quality of the stitching. It should be even and firm with no sign of fraying or loosening. Leather should not have *any* cracks at all in it. The top, or smooth side, of the leather (which shows the natural pores and creases of the skin it is made from) should be smooth and pliable, although new tack is invariably stiffer than well-cared-for, used tack, while the underneath may be paler and have less of a sheen to it. Poor-quality tack often looks rough or bitty on the under side, whereas good-quality leather is

Look for these two logos to be sure of expertise and fair dealing.

smooth and well waxed, although this is not an infallible guideline.

It is not always easy to distinguish good fabrics and textiles from bad, but if you buy a reputable brand name and take good advice you should not go far wrong. Again, always check the quality of the stitching and finish and the apparent strength of the article.

Metal items like bits and stirrups should always be made of stainless steel, although you will find that other patented metals are now coming out which claim to be just as strong. Never buy metal described as 'solid nickel'. This is very weak: it bends, cracks, wears and breaks fairly easily and can cause nasty accidents. Riding is a strenuous sport and the safety and quality of your equipment could make the difference between being killed or staying alive. Nickel has a yellowish tinge to it and should be stamped or labelled as such, as, indeed, should whatever other metal you buy. If you are considering metals other than nickel or stainless steel, check with the retailer about their qualities and reliability.

You may see bits with copper inserts or mouthpieces. I am not in favour of these. Copper is a very soft metal and although a reputable manufacturer would not use it in a situation where it would have a lot of wear, as on a joint, the 'good mouthing properties' it is said to possess only come about because it tastes absolutely revolting , so that the poor animal champs the bit and salivates in an effort to get rid of the nauseating taste! Surely this is not something any caring owner would wish to subject their horse to.

Buckles, such as those on bridles and rugs made of traditional, as opposed to synthetic, materials, are often a source of problems. Stainless steel buckles are ideal but often we see good items fitted with nickel buckles that wear and break. Whenever you can, try to insist on stainless steel buckles on your tack.

Throughout this book, emphasis is placed on good design and fit. It has to be said, however, that many of the people currently designing tack and clothing for horses and ponies do not actually have much practical experience of them and often do not fully appreciate the minutiae of their conformation and action. Reputable manufacturers often consult experienced horsepeople over the design of their lines, usually famous international riders, but they still produce items that are extremely well made, of high-quality materials and superb workmanship but not appropriate to an animal of the make and shape of a horse. This is particularly true with rugs, although great improvements have recently been made in this field.

Saddles are another area where design is not always what it should be. Sometimes very expensive, beautifully made saddles can be difficult to fit to the most normally shaped horse and be significantly uncomfortable for the rider, too.

Once you have found a well-designed, soundly made article, you still have to fit it to your horse, and perhaps to yourself, too. To be useful and safe, tack and clothing have to be comfortable for the horse and not cause him any discomfort, pain or anxiety whatsoever.

The importance of well-fitting tack
Apart from being cruel intentionally to cause the horse pain, the horse's mentality has a lot to do with the importance of fit. The horse is a prey animal. He has a natural fear of confinement, constraint and pain. Whereas a hunter animal, such as a cat, dog or human, may try to reason with discomfort, either putting up with it or trying to get round it, a horse, depending on his personal temperament, will often simply panic. His evolved mentality is one that is used to freedom and being able to run away from danger. For example, if he is wearing a saddle that digs in or a girth that rubs, a noseband that almost stops him breathing or a bit that actually hurts him, he may begin to get angry or frightened and then panic and fight. This is where *our* problems really start, because an animal as strong as a horse, or even a tiny pony, is extremely dangerous when panicking because it can easily become out of control. Fear-stricken horses do not think about what they are doing or where they are going. They have evolved to gallop full tilt and 'blindly' away from whatever is causing them danger or pain, and this is what many of them try to do when hurt or subjected to serious discomfort from their tack. They will then fight their riders or handlers and no human is capable of effectively controlling a horse in such a state by ordinary means.
Design and fit are, therefore, not merely matters of desirability and practicality but of safety, too.

Another aspect of safety is dependent on something already mentioned – good quality. Cheap, weak or badly put-together items are prone to excessive wear or may break without warning. Imagine how dangerous it could be if, for example, your girth breaks while you are galloping across country, your bit breaks because of some unusual pressure you have put on it, perhaps because your horse took an awkward jump, or your stirrup leather gives way as you land after a jump. Falls and injuries can happen in this way, not to mention lives being lost.

Good-quality materials will have been tested for strength before being incorporated into tack or clothing. The new synthetic materials that are now more widely used for tack and clothing are often scientifically developed and tested to recognized standards before being made available to manufacturers.

Where economy is a serious consideration, it is far preferable and safer to buy really good-quality second-hand equipment than poorer-quality new gear for a similar price. If you really do prefer new tack, and of course most of us do, paying a seemingly high price for good quality is, in fact, good economy. If you care for the item properly and use it wisely, you will still be getting valuable use out of it many years after you have forgotten how much it cost.

CHAPTER 2

THE
TACK ROOM

Correct storage is one of the most important factors in keeping your tack and other equipment in good condition. Tack is expensive and it pays to look after it. It is also valuable to thieves, so security of the tack room is as important as its suitability.

Leather, most traditional fabrics and many synthetics will keep better if stored in dry, reasonably warm conditions. The atmosphere in a tack room should not become humid and should ideally be maintained at around room temperature of about 20°C. It is true that many tack rooms have no heating of any kind, but because the tack is in regular use and properly cleaned and cared for it does not really suffer.

A well-kept tack room, with bridles hung from semi-circular brackets and saddles on modern, plastic-covered brackets, correctly placed with the pommels facing the wall. Two saddles are ready for cleaning. The one on the right has had the stirrups and girth removed.

However, tack rooms with some form of heating (ideally a thermostat-operated heater that will keep the air at a constant temperature round the clock) certainly keep tack in super condition, provided it is also well cared for, and are pleasant to work in.

Excessively hot, dry surroundings are almost as bad as cold, damp ones. Heat will dry out and crack leather (although fabrics may not suffer) wheras cold and damp conditions will cause both leather and fabrics to become mouldy and, in some cases, actually to rot.

FITTINGS AND RACKS

Your most valuable item of tack is likely to be your saddle, and good, supportive storage of this on a well-designed saddle rack is important in helping it to retain its shape and, therefore, fit. Do not store your saddle on a single pole or rope which reaches up inside the gullet, as this will stretch the seat from underneath. Proper saddle racks, which support the saddle on the underseat, stuffed panels, are the best but upturned-V racks or similarly shaped, free-standing saddle horses

Preventing theft

Many tack rooms are attached to stable blocks or are positioned somewhere in the stable yard. Provided they can be made secure as regards doors, windows *and* walls, this may be acceptable. Thieves are ever enterprising and dream up the most ingenious and daring ways to part you from your tack. Taking bricks and boards out of walls is nothing to them, nor is forcing doors, breaking windows and clipping out metal grilles on windows.

It is a good plan to ask the Crime Prevention Officer from your local police force to come and assess your premises as a whole and recommend security precautions for the whole yard, including the tack room. Normally, a door should have two mortise bolts and/or locks fitted and the type of hinges that are recessed and impossible to unscrew. Windows need strong metal bars that would be a lot of trouble to saw through and walls should be as strong as possible – if you have only one stone- or brick-built room on the yard,

for example, this should be used as the tack room if possible. Wooden buildings are fairly easy to saw into.

The best position for the tack room is inside, or attached to, the house (assuming the yard has living accommodation) as the occupants are then more likely to hear thieves working. It would then also be easy to attach the tack room to the house burglar-alarm system, if there is one. In any case, it should be well inside the yard so that access from outside is difficult or discouraging. Discouragement is the key to the whole matter! It is true that if thieves really want to steal your tack or your horses, they will, but the best you can do is make life as difficult as possible for them. In view of the fact that most people do *not* do this, you will be in a minority and the thieves are more likely to look for easier pickings elsewhere. Ideally the tack room should be handy for the stables, but security is really more important than practicality in this case.

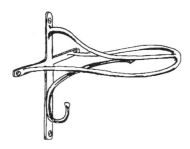

A good type of plastic-covered saddle bracket.

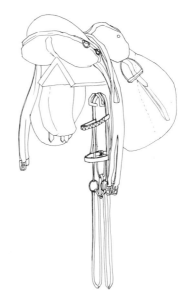

are just as good. The latter often have tops that turn over to hold the saddle so that you can clean the underside easily. They also have drawers at each end to hold tack-cleaning gear and a shelf underneath for boots or other equipment. Often fitted with wheels, they are very practical and convenient. Saddle racks can be fitted to the walls at a comfortable height for you to reach (probably just above your own head height), and are often combined with a bridle holder in one fitting.

If you have no saddle rack, it is perfectly satisfactory to stand the saddle on its pommel on the folded girth or a stable rubber or other means of protection (to avoid scratching, marking and weakening the leather) and the bridle can then be draped over the cantle. Make sure the cantle is protected from being scratched or split if it leans against a wall. A saddle rack will, however, be more convenient and will help the saddle to keep its shape better.

Your bridle can be laid over the saddle seat when the latter is on its rack but, again, most people prefer to have a bridle rack. This should be of the semi-circular (or circular) sort so that the bridle headpiece and the

Another good, older type of saddle bracket with bridle holder underneath.

noseband underneath it are kept in good shape. If you hang the bridle on a short pole or stick you will get a bend of the same shape in the

An old-fashioned saddle horse supports the saddle well for cleaning and has drawers and a shelf for equiptment, boots etc.

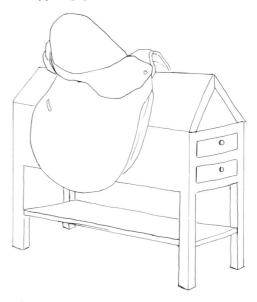

leather, and if you do even worse and hang it on a nail or hook you will actually encourage the leather to bend sharply and crack, which may eventually cause it to break.

Rug racks of some sort are useful for both storing and airing rugs. Once aired, they can be folded and stored on shelves, in deep drawers or in chests or trunks stored a little way off the floor just in case of water seepage or flooding at some time, or someone knocking over a bucket of water when cleaning tack.

There are racks that fold back flat against the wall: the rug is fastened at the breast and hung from the breast strap and also supported at the withers so that it hangs downwards, in shape, for airing and storage. However, certainly one of the most practical ways of airing rugs is on an old-fashioned clothes rack that can be hauled up on a pulley system to the roof or ceiling. Because heat rises, in a room kept reasonably warm even thick rugs of traditional woollen fabric, or wet canvas turnout

rugs, will dry relatively quickly with this arrangement. These racks also have the advantage of keeping the clothing up above your head and out of your way, assuming the ceiling is high enough.

Storage space
Chests of drawers, shelving and cupboards are all useful in tack rooms, which invariably become a general storage area for all the paraphernalia that finds its way into a yard. Boots and bandages, spare bits, tack-cleaning gear, grooming kits, whips, hard hats, gloves, books and also the yard first aid kit (which should be kept in a lockable cupboard) are all normally to be found in the tack room and it is easy for it to become really untidy very quickly. A good discipline to get used to is 'Don't put it down, put it away', then you will never have to tidy up! One boring job avoided!

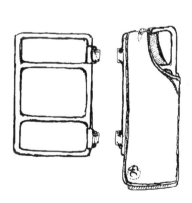

Modern rug bracket which screws to the wall by means of hinges.

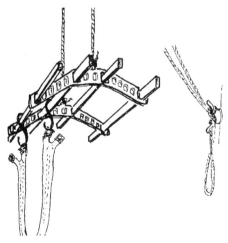

A boon to any yard is this old type of clothes airer.

WATER AND POWER

A tack room with a laid-on water supply is by far the most convenient, although it is possible to manage by carrying buckets of water from elsewhere. Certainly, it is a good idea to have an electric socket so that you can boil a kettle (for warming tack-cleaning water or making coffee). An instant, wall-fitted, electric water heater is a boon fitted over a sink or other outlet, as this makes it easy to rinse through synthetic boots, bandages and over-reach boots, etc. Anything that needs a proper wash is probably best put through a washing machine and in larger yards this, too, might be sited in the tack room.

CLEANING TACK

Tack-cleaning equipment can easily become messy and should not be left lying around with the soap exposed to dirt and grit (which is later transferred to your leather during cleaning, thus scratching it), and the same goes for your soap sponge. It should be kept in a drawer or in some sort of 'tidy' or carrier on a shelf, probably covered, like your grooming kit, with a stable rubber or old tea-towel. Leather dressings are invariably liquid oils of some kind and should have their tops firmly screwed on after use. The brushes that go with them must be kept free of dirt and grit. Brushes, dressings and oils are most usefully stored on shelves. Buckets should be rinsed out after use and allowed to drain and dry, perhaps on a draining board or outside upside down, then stored, again upside down, to keep the insides clean, on shelves in the tack room.

That useful old saying –'a place for everything and everything in its place' except when it is being used – will help you to keep track of what can easily become a very messy area. With good storage facilities, however, and a comfortable atmosphere, you will find your tack room kind to both your tack and yourself.

CHAPTER 3

SADDLES AND RELATED ITEMS

The art of saddle making is an ancient one and although the development of the saddle did not run concurrently among ancient peoples, various aspects of design kept cropping up quite independently in various parts of the world where horses were used. Originally it was just an animal skin thrown over the horse's back and we still mostly use animal skin today. However, synthetic materials are now becoming well established in the saddlery trade and some excellent wholly or partly synthetic saddles (and other tack) are available.

Until the 1950s, there were only two basic saddle designs to choose from in the UK – the old-style hunting saddle and the side-saddle. Other types, such as children's saddles in various styles, such as felt-pad saddles and basket saddles for tiny tots, and specialized showing saddles and racing saddles were available in their fields.

Then, in the mid-1950s, show jumping and general purpose saddles began to be widely available, followed soon afterwards by dressage saddles, and gradually the old hunting saddles started to go out of use as people realized how much more practical and comfortable the newer

designs were and how much easier it was to ride in a balanced seat in them.

Today, those three basic types – the general purpose, jumping and dressage saddles – have been joined by variations within their types and also by endurance riding saddles. Of course, side-saddles, showing and racing saddles are still available but it is extremely difficult now to get children's pad saddles and I cannot remember the last basket saddle I saw!

CONSTRUCTION

Saddles are traditionally constructed on a laminated beechwood frame called a tree. The shape of the tree determines the style of the saddle and, therefore, how the rider rides in it and for what purpose it is suitable. Nowadays, trees are also made of synthetic materials of various sorts and these have the advantage of being very light and hardwearing and are also less prone to cracking if dropped. Some early synthetic trees tended to spread out of shape but this fault seems to have been overcome with later models. Some trees have lengthwise metal strips or blades attached to them to give added comfort to the rider: these are called 'spring' trees, the others being called 'rigid' trees. Once you are used to a spring-tree saddle, rigid trees are very hard and unforgiving no matter how well padded the seat is and they rarely seem to be used these days except in children's saddles. Spring-tree saddles are more expensive but I cannot imagine anyone thinking the extra expense is not worthwhile.

The front and back arches (the pommel and cantle, respectively) are reinforced by the addition of metal plates, and the all-important stirrup bars are riveted onto the tree. A new development is stirrup bars that can be adjusted backwards or forwards to suit the rider and the seat he or she wishes to adopt, either a longer-leg position for dressage, which needs the stirrup bar to be nearer the rider's seat bones in the lowest part of the

saddle seat, or a more forward position for the shorter-stirrup seats used in jumping or active hacking.

Some newer designs of saddle can actually have the width of the tree adjusted, within certain limits, with a view to making them adjustable to the changing shape and muscling of a horse's back throughout a year when his workload, and therefore his muscular development and fitness, alter due to his programme. This also means that one saddle can be made to fit several horses, a factor that is very useful for large yards. However, some designs require the saddle to be adjusted by a saddler, which is not so convenient, although others can be adjusted at home by the owner.

The tree will have various additions such as fabric coverings, padding and webbing (or synthetic) strips for the attachment of the vital girth straps. Finally the leather covering is added.

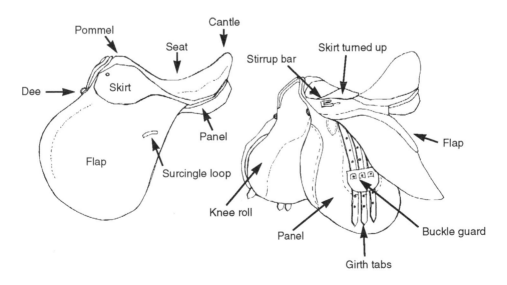

The parts of the saddle.

SHAPE AND BALANCE

The key to all good riding is balance. If the rider is not in harmonious balance with his or her horse so that they truly move with him and work with his movements rather than against them, no amount of sympathetic rein handling or subtle aid application will do much good. The horse was not designed to be ridden. The fact that his back is comfortable for people to sit on is a fortunate fluke of nature. His backbone is designed to carry weight slung underneath it (in the form of his heavy intestines and other abdominal contents) rather than on top of it but its structure is so strong that the horse can carry reasonable amounts of weight with little difficulty over long distances and at high speeds provided he is physically fit to do so and the rider rides well. A horse should be able to carry about one-seventh of his own weight (including saddle and rider) depending on his individual constitution and the rider's skill.

FITTING A SADDLE

The horse's centre of gravity is normally said to be in the centre of his body at a point just behind the elbow, about a third of the way up his body from the sternum or breast-bone. The object in fitting and balancing a saddle to suit a particular horse is to arrange things so that the lowest part of the dip in the saddle seat is directly over the horse's centre of gravity *and* in the centre of the saddle seat when viewed from the side. The stirrup leathers should

The horse's back

If you look at a horse from the side with no saddle on, you will notice that his back appears to dip slightly from behind the withers, rising gently again to the croup (the highest point of the hindquarters). However, if you look at the skeleton of a horse and note the actual line of the vertebrae that make up his spine, you will see that the spine does not, in fact, dip downwards but is slightly arched upwards. The apparent dip in the back of a fully fleshed horse is caused by the differing lengths of the bony fingers (called processes) that protrude upwards from the top of each individual vertebra. As any mechanical engineer will tell you, this slightly arched structure is extremely strong and is the design regularly used in the construction of bridges and flyovers. Luckily for us, this means that we can expect our horses to carry suitable amounts of weight on their backs.

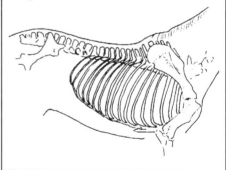

hang down vertically from the stirrup bars and may be sited near the dip or further forward according to the design of the saddle and its purpose, as already mentioned.

Seen from the back, the saddle should sit evenly on the horse's back, but it has to be said that if the horse

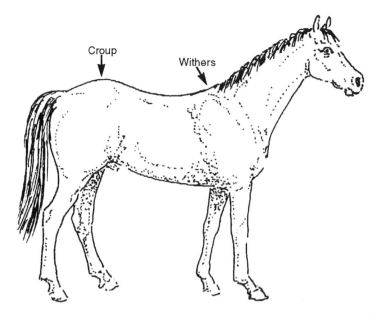

This horse's croup (the highest point of his hindquarters) is higher than his withers which makes saddle fitting difficult and causes an uncomfortable ride.

is unevenly developed due to a faulty way of going or bad riding or schooling, which all produce uneven development of the muscles, this may not be possible even if the saddle itself is perfect. A good saddler will, however, be able to adjust the stuffing in the underseat panel to compensate until matters are corrected in the horse himself.

When riding, most riders find that they naturally slip backwards a little in the saddle and periodically have to correct their position. Because of this, it is often found that many saddles, and particularly dressage saddles, have their cantles a little higher than their pommels to counteract the natural backward movement. However, the central dip is still important. If the pommel is too low and the dip too far forward, the rider will be thrown onto the

pommel (most uncomfortably); the same can happen in a horse with croup-high conformation, where his croup is higher than his withers. Although this conformation is common in young horses, say up to about four or five years of age (longer in some breeds and individuals), who will 'come up' in front later, in a horse of six years or over nothing can be done about it. The saddle will be constantly thrown forward with every stride, can dig in behind the horse's shoulders and can also give the rider a most unpleasant 'going-downhill-all-the-time' feeling.

The reverse conformation of very high withers, particularly if combined with a slab-sided horse or one in poor condition, can result in the saddle sliding back and a breastgirth or breastplate will be needed to keep it in place. Although a crupper (see

High, sharp withers, as here, usually mean you have to buy a saddle with a cut-back head or pommel in which the pommel is shaped out to accommodate the withers.

page 38) can help to keep a saddle back, when necessary, and was once often used on fat ponies, it is far from ideal and must be fairly uncomfortable for the animal even if the padded loop is kept soft and well oiled.

IMPORTANT FEATURES OF THE SADDLE

In most types of modern saddles the panels under the saddle flap have knee rolls of padded leather to provide support for the rider's knee and to help to keep their legs in the correct position. Knee rolls on general purpose/event and show jumping saddles are a real boon when landing after a jump. So-called thigh rolls, which are sometimes seen running vertically down the back of

the panel, are useless but those that run diagonally down and forwards, following the line of the under-thigh, sometimes found on dressage saddles, can be useful if the rider feels he or she needs help to maintain a good leg position.

The different stirrup lengths adopted for different disciplines determine how far forward the flap is cut. Obviously, the shorter your stirrups the more flexed or angled your legs will be and the further forward your knee will go, therefore you need a saddle that will comfortably accommodate your knee in the appropriate position. For general cross-country work, or hacking, the general purpose saddle has a moderately forward-cut flap, while the show jumping saddle has a more forward-cut flap to allow for the shorter stirrup often used for this

Underneath the flap of a saddle. The knee rolls help to stabilise the rider's leg but the thigh rolls on the back of this panel do not serve any useful purpose. This saddle has only two girth tabs instead of the normal three. There is nothing wrong with that but the leather flap over the tabs should be pulled right down over the buckles once the girth has been finally adjusted to prevent the buckles damaging the underside of the flap. The saddle is worn with a fleecy, padded numnah, the girth having been passed up through a loop on its bottom edge to help to keep the numnah in place. You can just see the strap of a breastplate at the pommel.

Under the flap of a dressage saddle, showing the knee roll and long girth straps. This saddle has no thigh roll behind the girth straps.

discipline (although the rather short stirrup style is not now so popular) and the dressage saddle has a straighter flap.

Dressage saddles are often also used for showing now as they are sufficiently straight-cut to show off the horse's front (the idea behind the very straight-cut showing saddles) yet give a much more comfortable ride to both exhibitor and all-important judge than traditional showing saddles. If the rider is comfortable, whatever the discipline, he or she must ride better and the horse should, therefore, feel more comfortable and go better. Saddlers often produce their own version of particular saddles and there is at present a modern, comfortable showing saddle on the market.

 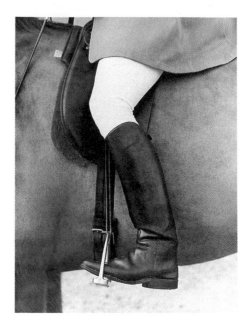

The rider's leg position on a jumping saddle, showing how the shorter length of leather causes more bend in the knee which can then be pressed into the knee roll (under the flap) for greater stability when jumping.

The rider's leg position on a dressage saddle. The leg is straighter than when jumping and a straighter-cut flap is used. Here the short dressage or belly girth is shown, fastening down below the saddle and thus removing any bulk under the flap which could interfere with the rider's close leg contact.

Some of the most comfortable saddles currently on sale are those designed for endurance riding, where riders are in the saddle for many hours. These saddles have well padded seats with Ds to attach the rider's equipment to en route, and, most important, they have a larger, wider bearing surface over the horse's back.

One of the important elements in fitting a saddle to the rider is that the saddle must not force the thighs uncomfortably far apart and this has, in the past, produced some designs where the waist or twist of the saddle (the narrowest part) has been unreasonably narrow when, in an effort to provide rider comfort, the area available to transfer weight to the surface of the horse's back has become smaller and smaller. The less area there is, the more weight must be concentrated onto that smaller area. The weight is the same but because it is borne on a small area it feels much heavier and more intense than if it were spread out. This cannot be comfortable for the horse and can, in practice, cause pressure injuries and, eventually, even deadened areas of skin and flesh,

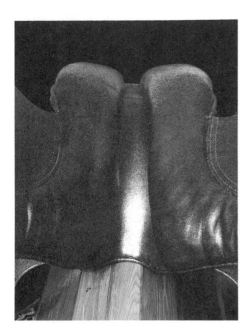 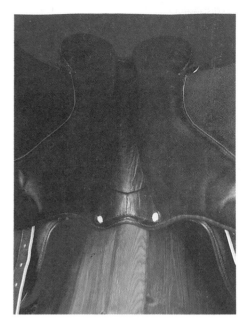

The underside of an endurance saddle, showing the much greater bearing surface which will spread the rider's weight more.

The underside of a jumping saddle, showing the fairly narrow waist or twist and, therefore the smaller bearing surface that will lie on the horse's back.

particularly if the stuffing of the saddle is uneven. These deadened lumps may need surgical removal.

Happily, the fashion for very narrow twists is now disappearing and a more comfortable width is usually available to help to spread the rider's weight

FITTING THE SADDLE TO RIDER AND HORSE

No matter how well designed the saddle, if it doesn't fit you both it is of no use. The most important point to remember as regards fitting the horse is that the saddle must not even touch, let alone press upon, the

horse's spine anywhere at all along its length when the horse's heaviest rider is in the saddle. The rider should ride round in the saddle without a numnah for about fifteen minutes to let it settle, tighten the girth again if necessary, and then lean right forwards and right back. An observer on the ground should be able to confirm that he or she can still see a clear tunnel of daylight down the horse's back with the rider in all of these positions.

Having taken care of that point, you must check that you can get at least three fingers' width between the withers and the underside of the pommel, and the same at the cantle. The rear of the saddle must rest on

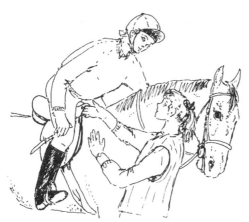

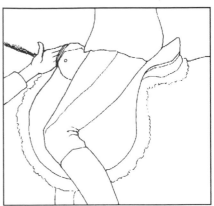

When the horse's heaviest rider leans forward, there should be three fingers' width between the underside of the pommel and the top of the withers.

You should be able to slide the flat of your fingers around the withers beneath the pommel.

the horse's back but must not press on the loins at all.

At the front you should just be able to slide the flat of your fingers under the pommel all round the withers to check for width. If the saddle is too narrow it will pinch; if too wide it will rock around and could bruise the withers. Also ask

your helper on the ground to lift the horse's foreleg from the knee and pull it right forward (the horse may need some gentle but persistent persuasion to do this) to check that the top of the shoulder blade is not pressed on by the saddle at the front, thus interfering with the horse's action and maybe bruising his shoulders.

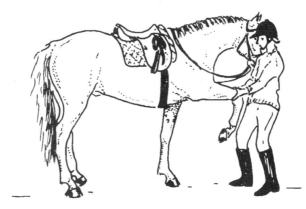

Bring out the horse's leg from the knee, getting him to extend the shoulder forward so that the top of his shoulder blade moves backwards. There should be no interference with its movement from the saddle, otherwise it will make the horse sore and interfere with his action, possibly making him resentful and unwilling. Never try to force the horse to lift his leg up from the ground straight by pulling up from the fetlock: the horse's anatomy makes this extremely uncomfortable for him. If you try, you will find that he has to partially bend his knee.

Size of the saddle

When the rider is seated normally and comfortably, he or she should be able to get the width of one hand in front of their body at the pommel and behind their seat at the cantle. The rider's leg and knee should be comfortably accommodated by the size and design of the flap. He or she should also feel that the thighs are not being pushed unreasonably far apart by the saddle. Of course, the saddle width depends largely on the width of the horse's back, so it is important that the rider and the horse fit each other too!

Saddles come in three normal widths – narrow, medium and wide – and go up to 17in (43cm) in length from pommel to cantle. (Few manufacturers use metric sizes). For most adults of average height and build a 16in (41cm) saddle is fine. It is sometimes possible to get 18in (46cm) or even 19in (48cm) saddles for large riders (who need a correspondingly substantial and longer-backed horse to carry them. A long back is a weak structure so the rest of the horse must have complementary confor-mation to counteract this.)

The rider is showing a good position for flatwork in a general purpose saddle. Concerning fit, from the rider's point of view the saddle would seem a little short, there being barely a hand's width in front of and behind him at pommel and cantle.

It has recently been realized by saddlers that female and male human pelvises are different, female pelvises being wider, among other things, than male ones. This has brought about the development of a special saddle specifically designed for female riders, which, in practice, is certainly extremely comfortable. There is also a saddle specially designed for classical equitation. This enables the seatbones and buttocks to spread over the seat of the saddle and the thighs to relax down the panels in the required position for classical equitation. Both these saddles have wider bearing areas for the horse's back without in any way forcing the thighs apart and causing the rider discomfort. Their very object is comfort for rider and horse. (The matter of the classical equitation seat being different from that used for 'ordinary dressage' always creates controversy and differences of opinion. The two disciplines are coming closer together these days but it remains a fact that some dressage riders do not use truly classical techniques in schooling. However, the discussion of this topic is outside the scope of this book.)

It is well worth keeping your eye on the equestrian press to see what further developments there may be in saddle design and manufacture.

STIRRUPS AND LEATHERS

Strong stirrup irons of the correct size for your foot and of a safe design are essential. If you have anything other than a basic plain iron (a simple English hunting iron, as it is

Checking the tree

The tree of a traditionally made saddle can be broken without much difficulty if the saddle is dropped or the horse and rider experience a fall. Synthetic saddles seem tougher in this respect.

To check the tree, grasp the pommel and cantle firmly in your hands and try to twist the saddle. Rest the cantle against your thighs and grasp the pommel with both hands and try to pull the pommel towards you. If, in either case, you feel or see movement or hear a grating sound, you can be pretty sure that the tree is well and truly broken. It is totally uneconomical to mend a tree (I'm not even sure it is possible to do it satisfactorily) and in future the saddle should only be used for demonstrating how to recognize a broken tree.

To ride a horse in a broken saddle should be considered a serious offence! It can cause severe pressure and, depending on the actual position of the break, maybe even a bad cut or bruise if the tree comes close enough to the panel leather or even through it.

Two advantages of synthetic saddles are that, although some designs may not last a lifetime like good traditional saddles, they are at least cheaper and also seem tougher when it comes to accidents.

called) you must make sure it does not place your foot, ankle and leg in a position that is uncomfortable for you. If you are in significant discomfort when you are riding, you cannot ride to the best of your ability and your horse may sense your discomfort and act accordingly. This situation can be dangerous.

The strongest commonly available metal for stirrup irons is stainless steel, which is the best metal for the reasons already given on page 13, but, unfortunately, there is still a lot of so-called 'solid nickel' around which should certainly be avoided as it is simply not strong enough.

Size

The base of the iron on the inside should be 2.5cm (1in) wider than the sole of your riding boot at its widest point. Anything wider could allow your foot to slip through the stirrup and anything narrower might cause your foot to become jammed. In either of these instances you might be dragged and either killed or seriously injured in a fall.

The eye of the stirrup (the slit in the top) should allow your chosen width of stirrup leather to run through it easily rather than catching on the sides: this can hamper easy adjustment when mounted and can distort and wear the leather itself.

The leathers come in various lengths, from children's to full size adult leathers. Your saddler should sell you the correct length of leather according to the size and type of saddle you have.

As for width, a leather that is too narrow can be uncomfortable across your shin and one that is too wide can simply look ugly. It is really a matter of personal choice. If you get leathers (and here again they may be synthetic) just wide enough to run through the eye of correctly sized stirrups, you should be all right.

Types of stirrups

There are various types of stirrups but probably the only types worth bothering with are the plain English hunting iron or some sort of safety iron such as the Peacock Safety Stirrup.

There are various other designs, most of which aim to 'persuade' your

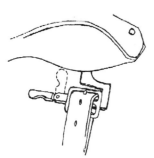

The safety catch on the end of the stirrup bar should be kept in the down position as shown. If there is an accident or fall the stirrup leathers will be pulled off the saddle and prevent you being dragged along. The up position (shown by the dotted line) was intended to release the leathers when pressure was applied to the catch but in practice, if the tack is not well-oiled, this often sticks.

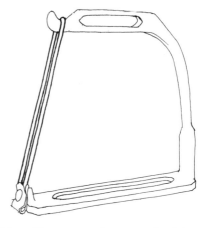

The rubber ring on the outer side of the Peacock Safety Iron releases if pressure is put on it from the foot, as in a fall, freeing the rider and helping prevent him or her from being dragged.

foot to go into a certain position (normally with your heel down and your toe to the front and maybe even also with the outside of your sole slightly lower than the inside) and while a few people swear by them I feel more probably ultimately discard them as being too forced and rigid for relaxed riding: as stated earlier, if you are not comfortable you cannot ride really well.

Types of leathers

If you want leather stirrup leathers, it is a good plan to buy what are known as red buffalo-hide leathers. These are often described as unbreakable and I have certainly never known one to break, not even old, neglected ones. The stitching (of the leather to the buckle) is a different matter.

Safety first

Your leathers are as vital to safety as your irons: *any* cracks, major or minor, in the leather, or any frayed or loose stitching, must be put right by the saddler at once. Badly worn pieces can be replaced but the repair will obviously need stitching and will subsequently require frequent checking. Most people discard worn leathers or use them for other purposes such as neckstraps for novices and children or for making rug breast straps, etc.

There are also ox-hide and rawhide leathers: all can be good if well cared for. Although buffalo-hide ones do stretch more easily than the others,

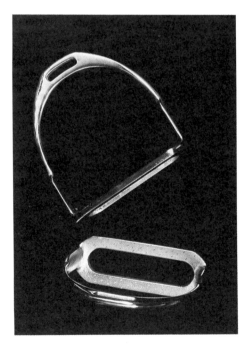

A standard English hunting stirrup iron.

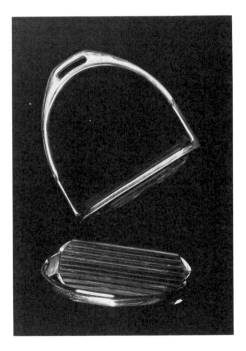

An English hunting iron with the rubber tread in place.

this is not really a drawback if you regularly change the left and right leathers over so that the strain normally taken by the nearside (left) leather when the rider mounts is borne by each leather of a pair in turn.

Again, make sure your leathers have stainless steel, high-quality buckles and never nickel ones. The buckle tongue should be firm but easily movable for ease of adjustment, and there should be a little nick in the top bar of the buckle for the tongue to rest in, which helps its stability.

When buying leathers, you may notice that the flesh ('rough') side of the leather is outermost and the smooth (grain) side on the inside; this is so that the smooth, stronger side will take the strain of the wear from the stirrup, which, as you can imagine, is considerable. This is not usually the case with buffalo-hide leathers, however, as the hide is so strong that it doesn't matter.

Very good-quality leathers will have the holes numbered and it is important: (a) that you make sure you get a real pair with holes and numbers corresponding all the way down; and (b) that you do change them over regularly so that they stretch evenly and remain matched as far as the distance between holes is concerned. Otherwise , you will never be able to get your leathers evenly adjusted and will always be riding lopsided.

To make sure they are even when you buy them, place the leathers 'back to back', put a matchstick or something similar through the top hole to keep them even, then put one through all the other holes all the way down in pairs. If you cannot do this easily do not buy them.

With a well-designed, modern saddle that has recessed stirrup bars (they nearly all have these days) you will not be troubled by bulky buckles under your thigh when you ride. However, to obviate any possibility at all of this, you can now buy leathers specially designed for dressage, which fasten at the stirrup iron rather than up under your thigh: the leather still slots over the bar but the buckle is down by your ankle. In any case, never pass the spare end of leather *under* the doubled part when you are mounted, as this creates a bulky fold under your thigh: just leave it on top, flat, and pass it behind your thigh. You will find that it will stay there quite naturally and should not cause you any problems, although if it is too long it may flap about and irritate your horse. If it is really getting in your way, you can pass the spare end through the surcingle loop on the saddle.

GIRTHS

The type and adjustment of the girth you use to keep your saddle on is vital to the comfort of your horse and to the security and safety of both of you. Again, there are leather and synthetic girths and also girths made from natural fabrics, such as lampwick, cotton and mohair.

Leather girths
Leather is very strong and long-lasting provided it is looked after (cleaned and probably oiled or

dressed regularly) but it is only slightly absorbent and, obviously, the areas beneath your saddle and girth can become very wet with sweat during any other than light work because the air cannot reach them to help with the evaporation of the sweat and the drying of the area.

Nevertheless, many people swear by leather girths and although they may be rather unforgiving, like a tight leather belt around your waist, they do not cause trouble if kept in good order and comfortably adjusted.

Natural fabrics

Natural fabric girths have the advantage of being softer and more comfortable and must have a little more 'give' in them than leather. They also absorb sweat and are cooler in summer. Again, though, if allowed to become hard with dried sweat and grease from the horse, they can cause problems, galling the horse and making him uncomfortable.

Cotton and woollen webbing

Two natural fabrics that are not particularly good are cotton and woollen webbing. Webbing girths are hard by nature and must be kept very clean and be well cared for if they are not to rub the horse. Cotton webbing girths, which are usually fairly narrow, have to be used in pairs as a belt-and-braces operation because they are so prone to snapping under stress! Woollen webbing girths, which are wider, can be used singly as they are stronger but in my view they are still rather harsh on the horse.

Very narrow, white, beige or brown showing girths are used in the

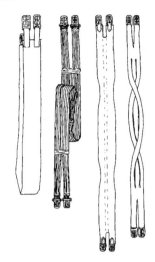

Different types of girth: from left, plain girth with elastic inserts at the buckles; string girth; Atherstone pattern; Balding pattern.

showring on children's ponies, and are all right for this short period if in good condition. These are made of cotton webbing and have a little section of pimpled rubber at the breastbone to help keep them in place.

Woollen webbing is often used for surcingles, which are fastened completely round the saddle, over the top, as an extra precaution, in addition to the normal girth, in cross-country competition such as eventing or team chasing.

Synthetic fabrics

Synthetic fabrics vary from straightforward nylon (not a good choice as it can be rough and is even worse for sweating than leather, being totally non-absorbent) to the various new permeable or 'breathable' fabrics that 'wick' (draw) moisture away from the horse through the fabric, allowing it to evaporate in the outside atmosphere. If you come home from a ride after using one of these girths you will notice how much drier your horse is than underneath other types of girth. Yet again, as with all tack, you need to keep them clean and in good repair if they are to remain safe and comfortable for the horse.

Styles of girth

Girths of all kinds can have elastic inserts in them to provide more give and thus more comfort for the horse. Of course, elastic is made of rubber which will perish eventually no matter how well you care for it but the inserts (one at each side of the girth to provide even tension) can be replaced by a saddler. It is also possible to get wholly elastic girths (usually worn for racing) but these can be difficult to adjust and are not really practical for everyday use.

There are girths made of strands of strings of various fabrics that have the aim of allowing air between the strands to help with the sweat problem. If of cotton or leather, these can work quite well, but avoid the nylon string girths as they do not work well in practice. String-type girths (except leather) have woven pieces set periodically along their length to help to prevent the strings bunching together, and these girths work fairly well.

Webbing surcingle (with elastic insert) secured over the saddle and girth and through the breast-plate loop, as used in cross-country work for extra safety and security. It is a very sensible belt-and-braces practice.

Recommended
U leather – especially Balding or Atherstone – must be kept clean and supple
U natural – all except woollen webbing or cotton webbing, provided they are kept clean
U synthetic – the 'breathable' new fabrics, provided they are kept clean

Not recommended
U natural – woollen webbing which can become hard and rub
     – cotton webbing which can snap under stress
U synthetic – nylon which is rough and does not allow sweat to evaporate
     – elastic – only for racing
     – nylon string – can rub

Types of girth
U leather
U natural – lampwick, cotton, mohair, wool
U synthetic – nylon and other manmade fabrics

Probably the two designs (available in various natural or synthetic fabrics) that are justifiably the most popular are the Balding and Atherstone girths. These are both shaped to be narrower behind the horse's elbow, the part where there is most movement and where girth galls occur. This shaping does make things more comfortable for the horse, giving him real 'elbow room' and allowing him to move freely without coming up against an uncomfortable restriction behind his elbow at every stride.

Short belly girths are designed for use with dressage saddles (some of which have correspondingly long girth tabs or straps to accommodate them) and have the aim of completely removing buckles from under the saddle flap and your leg. The idea is a good one but in practice the buckles often turn out to lie behind the horse's elbow, exactly where you do not want bulk, especially hard bulk like buckles. Because the buckles in a belly girth come below the bottom of the saddle panel and are therefore in contact with the horse himself, they need a protective piece of leather (or some other tough material) behind them to protect the horse and prevent possible pinching of his skin between the two buckles. This, too, creates extra, unwanted bulk just where it isn't wanted, so with belly girths it is often a case of 'out of the frying pan into the fire'.

Actually, the matter of getting rid of buckles beneath your leg without giving the horse extra problems is simple. Girths come in a wide variety of lengths and it is quite easy to get one of a suitable length so that,

when correctly adjusted, the buckles come under the saddle flap behind the crook of your knee, well out of harm's way and interfering neither with your leg nor the horse's elbow movement. When you are mounted, just ask a friend to measure from behind one of your knees, under the horse's breastbone where the girth will go and up to behind your other knee, then buy a girth of your choice in that length and your problem is solved.

As with any tack, it is best to ask for stainless steel, high-quality buckles on your girth, and if it does not come with these, to get them replaced. Any competent saddler can do this and it is well worth your trouble and the slight expense.

NUMNAHS AND SADDLE CLOTHS

Many people like to use some form of protective pad, however thin, under their saddle. If it is well fitted and permeable or absorbent, it does give extra comfort to the horse's back and draws away sweat. Wet skin is soft and can be more easily rubbed, resulting in possible soreness, and although well-cared-for tack should not cause any problems, using a good numnah or pad is a good precaution, if not essential.

Probably the most practical are the thin quilted-cotton numnahs shaped like a saddle and therefore available in various designs from dressage to show jumping styles. They are now even seen in the showring where once such things were really *infra dig!* These numnahs are absorbent and unobtrusive and provided their quilting is filled with cotton fibre rather than cheap plastic foam, are truly absorbent. The quilted nylon ones, either filled with nylon fibre or foam, are to be avoided. Synthetic fleece (usually acrylic) numnahs, about 2.5cm (1in) or so thick, with acrylic filling are popular and, although not as absorbent as cotton, really do pad the back if this is felt to be desirable. It should be remembered, though, that the thicker your numnah, the more chance the fit of your saddle will be significantly affected, so watch for this.

Natural sheepskin numnahs are less popular than they used to be as both they and acrylic pad-numnahs

Different numnahs and saddle cloths. At the top left you can just see the corner of a bound plain saddle cloth, on top of which are a fleecy, synthetic numnah, a synthetic quilted one, a nylon-covered foam-filled numnah (awful!) and a quilted saddle cloth.

can make the back rather hot and actually encourage sweating. You can get sheared sheepskin which is cooler. These days, sheepskin numnahs can often be washed in the washing machine but check on this or you might ruin a quite expensive item. The full sheepskin can also knot with friction and wear so you may have to comb it out carefully and regularly, depending on the type of hide used.

Proprietary saddle pads
There are various branded numnahs and saddle pads on the market with different claims and aims, most designed to wick away moisture from the back, and some designed to even out pressure through the various shock-absorbing qualities of their fillings. These can certainly be useful for sports such as endurance riding or any activity where the rider is mounted for long periods. You must care for these strictly in accordance with the maker's instructions or you could ruin them.

Therapeutic numnahs and pads
Numnahs and pads are available that claim to have actual healing properties in cases of back injuries such as bruising or muscle strain. With any such injury, after excess heat has subsided, usually after the first 48 hours, the aim is normally to provide gentle heat to keep the circulation flowing freely to the area, so promoting healing. These numnahs usually claim to have heat-retaining qualities which encourage the circulation and so promote healing. Polystyrene-filled pads (and also rugs) claim to act by providing an

opposite electrical charge to that given out by the body, which has a healing effect on soft tissues. 'Warm-up' numnahs (again heat-retaining) help to warm up horses before exercise, working on the principle that if a horse is worked too hard before his muscles have warmed up, those muscles might be more easily injured, a not-unreasonable supposition, and owners of athletic horses (and which working horse isn't really asked to do athletic work?) buy them for this purpose. Again, rugs and exercise sheets in similar fabrics are also available.

Numnahs

∪ Recommended – thin quilted cotton filled with cotton fibre
– synthetic 'breathable' fabrics

∪ OK – natural sheepskin – can encourage sweating, bulky, needs good care
– sheared fleece is better
– synthetic – can encourage sweating and be bulky

∪ Not recommended – thin quilted cotton filled with plastic foam
– quilted nylon filled with nylon fibre or foam

BREASTPLATES

Breastplates fasten either to the little metal rings or Ds on either side of the pommel and to the girth at the breastbone, fitting rather like a collar round the base of the neck, or can have a single strap going over the withers, holding up a broader band of leather or some other fabric which fastens at each end round the girth or round the girth tabs on the saddle under the saddle flap at each side.

They are useful for very fit, fined-down horses or those with big fronts or slab-sided conformation, whose saddles are prone to slipping backwards when the horse works. Breastplates can also, of course, be used to keep the saddle forward if the horse is in poor condition, but such horses should not really be worked until good condition has been regained.

NECKSTRAPS

Looking rather like the first type of breastplate described above, these are most useful for children or novice riders to hang on to to help them to keep their balance. They are not a sign of a poor rider but of a sensible one! It is a very bad fault in horsemanship to hang on by means of the reins or to be so insecure in the saddle that you constantly jab the horse in the mouth. A neckstrap is a wise and kind precaution.

The only real difference between a neckstrap and a breastplate is that the former does not have a fastening between the forelegs to the girth.

CRUPPERS

Cruppers are rarely seen on ridden horses these days and only occasionally on children's ponies. They are, however, still an integral part of a driving harness. On a driving horse they are fastened to a D on the cantle and consist of a leather strap with a thickly padded loop that goes

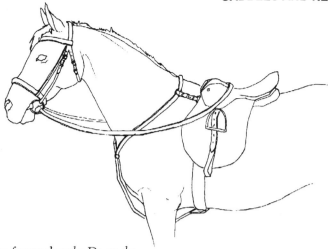

A breastplate fastened to the Ds on the saddle and round the girth.

under the horse's tail.

Their purpose is quite simply to keep the saddle in place on horses with poor fronts (shoulders) or with a 'downhill' or croup-high conformation, where the withers are lower than the highest part of the hindquarters. In such cases the saddle usually works forwards during work and can cause sore muscles behind the shoulders and encourage girth galls no matter how careful you are. Cruppers are also used on fat ponies whose gross bellies also force the saddle forwards. Occasionally, you will get a horse with exceptionally well-sprung ribs (a rounded ribcage). Even when in good condition and with otherwise good conformation, such a horse may benefit from a crupper.

It is particularly important that the tail loop part of the crupper is kept very clean and soft, as galling of the bare, thin skin around the root of the tail is otherwise quite easy.

A breastgirth which is supported by a strap over the withers and fastens round the girth under the saddle flap.

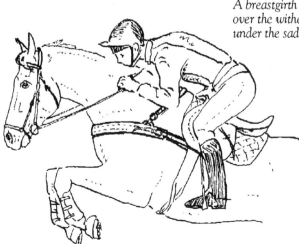

CHAPTER 4

BRIDLES

Early civilizations often controlled their horses, after a fashion, with a simple rope around the neck, as shown in various ancient carvings, bas-reliefs and paintings. Anyone who has ever tried to lead a less than perfectly willing, sensitive horse with a rope, or reins, around the middle to lower part of the neck will know it is not the most efficient way of doing this! It cannot have taken long before people realized that the higher up the neck you placed your rope, rawhide thong or whatever, the more control you had.

Ropes round the throat seem to have been used for a long time and it is only a short step from these to placing the rope around various parts of the animal's head, finding out by trial and error where it went best, where it would stay and where and how it offered most control.

It is perfectly possible to ride a horse in a bitless headstall, of course, as many people do today, but early man must have found that something in the mouth – initially probably a rawhide strip, later bone or wood, subsequently various metals –gave even more control and initiated more respect from most horses.

Today, other than in Western riding and its related schools, we have five basic types of bridle classified according to the type of bit

they carry. These are **snaffle** bridles, **double** bridles (comprising a curb bit and a small snaffle), **Pelham** bridles, **gag** bridles and **bitless** or nose bridles.

SNAFFLES

The snaffle is probably the most widely used bit and is the simplest in operation. It has a very direct 'feel' or action on the horse's mouth because it has a ring directly attached to each end of the mouthpiece, to which the reins and the bridle cheekpieces are fastened. Some types have a metal bar (called the bit cheek) running down through each end of the mouthpiece, to which rings are attached instead. The purpose of cheeks is to help to prevent the bit being pulled through the mouth, which can happen with a green (unschooled) or difficult horse, or one out of control for some reason.

The rings themselves can be fastened to the mouthpiece, either by passing through a simple hole in the end of the mouthpiece or by means of what is called an eggbutt joint (because of its slightly bulging shape). The eggbutt joint passes a little way up and down the ring to prevent the corners of the horse's lips being pinched painfully between the

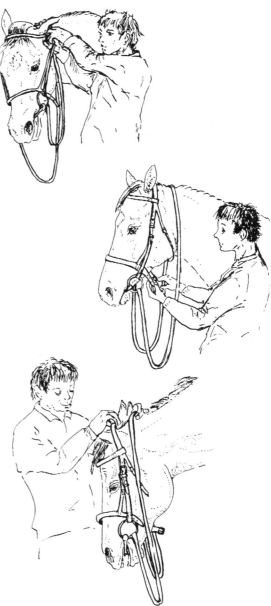

Putting on and taking off the bridle, from top left clockwise: You can hold the bridle as shown, or with your arm over the neck by the top of the headpiece, supporting the bit in your left hand and pressing it lightly where the teeth meet. Most horses will open their mouths and you can slide the bit carefully in. If they don't, insert your thumb in the corner of the horse's mouth (there are no teeth there) and tickle his tongue, which should do the trick.

Next, bring the bridle upwards, raising the bit in the mouth, and gently and quickly slip the headpiece over one ear at a time. If you leave the reins just behind the ears as shown, you can quickly get hold of them and control the head if he moves away. If you put them back on the withers you lose this form of control.

Next, fasten the throatlatch so that you can fit the width of four fingers between it and the head, then fasten the noseband to allow one finger comfortably under it all round.

Make the mane and forelock comfortable under the headpiece, bringing the forelock out over the browband, which should be roomy around the base of the ears, and see that the noseband and the bit lie evenly. The bit should touch the corners of the mouth but some experts recommend that it should create one wrinkle here.

To remove the bridle, undo the noseband and then the throatlatch, hold the buckle end of the reins and bring it up to the ears, then carefully slide the whole thing off and down over the ears. Allow the horse to open up and drop the bit in his own time. Never pull it out or snatch it out as this can really hurt him. If he won't let go use the thumb technique again.

ring and the hole in the mouthpiece, although in a well-fitting bit in good condition this almost never happens. In the other, loose-ring, arrangement, the rings slide round and back a little through the holes, and this gives a looser, freer feel to the bit which many horses prefer. The egg-butt, on the other hand, gives a more rigid, firm feel which can encourage some horses to lean on the bit a little (or a lot) and 'deaden' their mouths, whereas movement of the loose rings through the holes encourages salivation which keeps the mouth wet and more sensitive, or so the theory goes. In practice, this does seem to work, but all horses vary considerably in their preferences and you have to find these out by trial and error with different bits.

With rings that pass directly through the mouthpiece ends, you can use flat rings or rounded ones. Strictly speaking, flat rings are called loose rings and rounded ones, particularly when they are quite large to help to prevent them being pulled through the mouth, are called wire

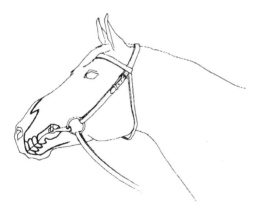

It is very convenient for us that there is a toothless gap in the horse's mouth at the corners of the lips, where the bit can lie.

rings but many people do not differentiate between them. If you ask a saddler for one or the other, however, he will know immediately what you want.

The snaffle mouthpiece can be quite varied, but basically there are: (1) jointed or 'broken' mouthpieces; (2) mullen or half-moon mouthpieces; and (3) straight-bar mouthpieces – with all sorts of weird and wonderful (or not so wonderful) inventions in between, all claiming miracles. Although it is true of any bit that the real criterion by which to judge its success is the skill and sensitivity of the hands at the other end of the reins (and the brain controlling them!) an explanation of the basic mechanics of the most common mouthpieces is necessary. I should point out that bitting itself has been made into a very complicated subject on which hefty volumes have been written. At its simplest, the theory is that the mouthpiece is used to apply pressure in and immediately around the horse's mouth; i.e., on his lips, which signals to the horse that the rider or driver wants him to do something – turn right, turn left, stop, raise his head, lower it and so on. It is also used to mean 'come to attention'; or, usually when pressure is released altogether, 'relax'. Of course, the horse must be trained to understand these signals and to train a horse requires an intelligent, truly 'thinking', sympathetic human, something that all too many horses do not have the benefit of when being schooled.

Unfortunately, because the horse has such a stupendous memory, he can recall without fail every unpleasant thing that happens to him as well as the good ones. This means that if the trainer is not particularly good and frightens, confuses or hurts the horse by their actions or even their verbal requests, the horse will remember and, largely because he is a prey animal with a well-developed sense of self-preservation and self-defence, will invent all sorts of major and minor ruses and techniques to protect himself.

Where the bit is concerned, this is called 'evading the bit'. To evade the action of the bit, the horse may raise or lower his head, poke his nose, bring it in towards his chest, cross his jaw, open his mouth, get his tongue over the bit, manipulate the bit into various positions in his mouth or, where all these fail or result in more pain and fear, will start to become more or less violent – napping and jibbing, running backwards, rearing, bucking, charging off or, less alarmingly, sidling around, going unwillingly and being generally 'sulky' and uncooperative. He will almost certainly become unresponsive to the bit and may lean on it, rake at the reins, bore or even develop a 'hard mouth' if the rider resists these efforts with a hard, unremitting contact.

In an ideal world all this would be avoided by expert schooling from the start: unfortunately, this often does not happen, and the vast variety of bits that are available is simply people's efforts to come up with ways of counteracting the horse's evasions in the absence of the riding skill needed. A skilled rider may need nothing more than a simple snaffle and, later, a double bridle in his or her tack room to school a horse to the highest standards. I know of one who does not use snaffles at all but begins every animal in a mullen-mouthed Pelham ridden on the curb rein only, and progresses to a standard double bridle as the horse's education reaches higher levels. His horses go beautifully and calmly.

However, snaffles remain the most popular bit for starting young horses and for sports such as show jumping, certain phases of eventing, endurance riding, lower-level competitive dressage and hunting, not to mention hacking.

The straight-bar snaffle
At its simplest, the straight-bar snaffle acts almost entirely on the tongue and lips. The horse can move the mouthpiece around with his tongue, but the straight bar does not leave much room for the tongue to lie comfortably beneath it, and this is a major drawback for an animal with a large, fleshy tongue.

The mullen-mouth or half-moon snaffle
The mullen-mouthed or half-moon mouthpiece is normally felt to be kinder in this respect: it does leave tongue room but this means the horse cannot move it about quite so much, nor lift it, therefore it puts more pressure on the bars of the mouth (those toothless gum areas inside the corners of the lips which seem to have been tailor-made to hold a bit!) The bars are bone, very thinly covered by flesh, and have a generous nerve supply. Although some horses have fleshier bars than others, no horse is born with a hard

mouth. An uneducated one may seem to have, but it is up to the trainer to school the horse to respond to light pressure rather than heavy.

The jointed snaffle

The jointed mouthpiece with a single joint bears more on the bars and lips. When the bit is used, the joint forms a marked V-shape which gives room for the tongue and makes it fairly difficult for the horse to move the bit around. As the bars are more sensitive than the tongue, a jointed mouthpiece is said to be 'stronger' (more severe) than a mullen or straight-bar one. In fact, if a single-jointed mouthpiece is used at all harshly, the joint can easily be pressed up into the sensitive roof of the horse's mouth and really hurt him by severely bruising this area. In coming up outside the mouth it can also crush the cheeks between the bit and the back teeth, causing a severe cut, so you can see that a snaffle, particularly a jointed one, is not necessarily a 'mild' bit at all, depending on how it is used.

The double-jointed snaffle

A double-jointed mouthpiece usually has a little flat spatula or link in the middle of the mouthpiece. It acts on the bars and lips and leaves less room for the tongue than a single-jointed bit and, depending on the angle of the spatula or link, the latter can press downwards into the tongue, creating a severe, even painful, feel for the horse. A very mild form is a French snaffle; a rather severe form is the Dr Bristol.

Less equals more!
Of course, the reason horsemen want a stronger feel is to get the horse to pay attention to their aids and obey them; in other words they wish to call the horse 'to heel' if he is ignoring mild, gentle aids. With some horses this works but with many the stronger and more painful the aid that is applied, the more they will resist and play up. Very often it is best to resort to a milder bit when experiencing problems, rather than a stronger one.

Whatever type of snaffle you buy, you should get one with a smooth mouthpiece. Old fashioned ones with 'rough' (sometimes even sharp) mouthpieces of various kinds, such as the twisted snaffle, are unnecessary and can certainly be classed as cruel in average hands.

CURBS AND DOUBLE BRIDLES

The curb bit works on a less direct principle than the snaffle, by means of leverage mainly on the horse's lower jaw but also slightly on his poll. A curb bit looks rather like a letter H with the horizontal bar too high up. The bridle has a separate headstall which fastens to the rings on the tops of the short, upper branches of the vertical cheeks, and the curb reins fasten to the rings on the bottoms of the lower branches.

When pressure is put on the curb reins by the rider, the bit cheeks are pulled backwards from the bottom. In addition to the bit mouthpiece, there is a chain called the curb chain, fastened by means of hooks hanging from the rings on the upper branches, going under the horse's lower jaw and lying in his curb groove or chin groove, as illustrated opposite. As the bit cheeks move backwards at the bottom they also have to move forward at the top but by a shorter distance because of their shorter length. This action tightens the chain against the horse's lower jaw and holds it all round in a gentle or harsher grip between the bit mouthpiece and the chain. The mouthpiece will act on the tongue, bars and lips and the chain in the chin groove. In addition, the short branches exert a downward pull on the top of the curb headstall which creates a similar downward pressure on the poll, encouraging the horse to lower his head.

The purpose of the all-round grip on the lower jaw is to ask the horse to 'give' or relax his lower jaw and poll and bring his nose back towards him so that, in a fully schooled horse, he will be going with the front of his face almost vertical to the ground. In this position, the bars of his mouth are most easily contacted by the curb mouthpiece so that the bit operates most effectively. (When a horse pokes his nose or goes with it significantly in front of the vertical, any bit will operate more on the corners of the lips, depending on how it is adjusted, rather than on the more sensitive bars, and is not, therefore, so effective.)

However, there is an important point to understand about the leverage principle on which curbs operate. The pressure a rider puts on the curb rein is multiplied several times in the horse's mouth. The leverage principle was used by ancient peoples

With the double bridle, the bridoon (small snaffle) lies where an ordinary snaffle does, with the curb about an inch below it. The curb here is a little too high. In the mouth, the bridoon lies over the curb. The curb chain goes behind the jaw, lying flat in the chin groove, passing between the curb and bridoon. A lip strap is also in use here.

to move massive boulders that they had no hope of shifting otherwise. It can also be seen in operation when a burglar forces a door with a crowbar: the pressure actually 'felt' by the door is much greater than that exerted by the burglar and will successfully force open a door that would be impossible to move otherwise. As far as the horse's sensitive, living mouth is concerned, this means that the pressure felt by his lower jaw will actually be four or five times greater than that exerted by the rider on the curb rein. It is for this reason that curb bits are regarded as 'strong', but they can and should be extremely gentle when used as intended by a skilled rider wishing to give his or her horse the lightest nuance of an aid and thus contributing to lightness and obedience in their mount.

Curb bits (also called Weymouths) can have straight or ported mouthpieces – a port being a little hump or 'bridge' in the mouthpiece to allow room for the tongue – or mullenmouthed for the same purpose. With a low or medium height port, there is room for the tongue and the ends of the mouthpiece are brought to bear on the bars. With a very high port, however, the top of the port can press on the roof of the mouth (as with a jointed snaffle) and really hurt the horse.

Western bridles often have curb bits with very high ports and are sometimes used very harshly – you can readily see the panic-stricken looks on the faces of horses in Western films when the riders pull hard, saw or jab at the reins and the horses open their mouths wide in a desperate attempt to escape the pain of the port and the vice-like grip on their lower jaws. This is poor riding – you cannot call it horsemanship – at its worst and most cruel.

The reason a double bridle is so called is because it has two bits; in addition to the curb or Weymouth there is a small snaffle bit – small in type and design, not width, with a thinner mouthpiece than an ordinary snaffle. As with saddle design, the principle of pressure on a large or small area is the same. A thin mouthpiece concentrates the pressure on the bars, whereas a thicker one spreads it. Well-designed snaffles will have rather oval-shaped

mouthpieces to assist this. The small snaffle used with a double bridle, called a bridoon or bradoon, has to have a thin mouthpiece because you cannot expect the horse to be comfortable with two conventionally thick mouthpieces in his mouth. However, because the horse has, or should have, reached a high standard in his schooling before being asked to wear a double bridle, he should be able to respond to the lightest pressure on the mouthpieces of the bridle and the thinness of the bridoon should not cause him discomfort.

The reason for the two, differently acting mouthpieces is so that the rider can ride mainly on the bridoon but, at the same time apply light aids with the curb, aimed at asking the horse to flex at the poll and give to the bit: the horse, therefore, has to think about two different requests given at the same time, not to mention all the other signals transmitted by the rider through weight, legs, whip and voice. Who said horses are not intelligent?

The double bridle enables very light aids to be given and is still regarded as the ultimate bridle for educated riding. It is, however, quite possible to ride a horse in collection, light and responsive to the aids, in just a snaffle. The double bridle is simply the icing on the cake, that extra touch of finesse that puts the polish on the performance.

Curb chains

The type of curb chain used is important to the horse's comfort as the chain acts on a thin-skinned and

Collection

Head position in itself does not, of course, govern collection. The object is to have the horse moving in what is termed self-carriage or self-balance, moving forward with considerable thrust and impulsion from his hindquarters, bringing his hind legs well underneath his belly and carrying more weight on his hindquarters than he naturally would. The fact that the head and neck are raised somewhat, with the neck arched and the face carried just in front of the vertical, with the poll flexed and the jaw relaxed in the best position to accept bit aids, combined with the lowered quarters and way of going, means that the horse gives his rider a sort of 'power boat' feeling – energy surging forward from the back, the horse light and strong at the same time, responsive and conducting an easy two-way conversation with his rider via the bit or bits in his mouth. This posture and mental attitude take years of training but this is the way in which the horse finds it easiest to carry his rider and comply with his or her wishes. Attainment of this way of going is a combination of physical development and conditioning and mental education. It is certainly not achieved just by putting a double bridle on the horse: the double bridle simply aids the horse's education and helps to bring out the best in him once trained.

very sensitive area of the horse's head.

Chains that are termed 'single link' chains are very widely available but are not very comfortable. Then there are flat (shaped) link chains which, because they present a flatter feel to the horse, are more comfortable. The third kind, which are finer, double-link chains, form a sort of coarse, flat mesh and are probably the most comfortable. You can also buy leather and elastic curbs with chain links only at each end for attachment to the hooks, and felt-backed leather ones which are my favourites. The elastic curbs are somewhat of a puzzle as although the idea of 'give' in the chain may sound humane, it must make for a less precise feel and therefore a clumsier aid. You can buy rubber covers for metal curb chains, which will make them feel softer but are not, of course, as absorbent as felt. The chin groove often becomes sweaty and the outsides of the mouth and lips become wet with saliva. You can also have made up, or sometimes buy ready-made, little sheepskin or fabric chain sleeves.

Lip straps

At one time it was regarded as *de rigeur* to ride with a lip strap securing your curb chain but few people seem to bother with them nowadays.

Hanging down from the centre of the curb is a small, single link called the fly-link, through which the lip strap was passed; the strap then fastened at each end to the small eyes on the bit cheeks. The idea was that it stopped the chain turning over (which is almost impossible if it is correctly adjusted) and prevented the bit cheeks coming too far forward, making it easy for the horse to catch hold of them and avoid the action of the bit. This possibility is so remote that people seem to prefer to take a chance on it rather than fuss with a lip strap!

Perhaps one occasion on which a lip strap would be useful would be on a horse with longish jawbones or with a curb with fairly long upper branches. In both cases the chain might ride up and operate on the thinly-covered lower jawbones instead of in the groove itself, and a lip strap might help to reduce this. This can also happen with Pelham bits, discussed next.

PELHAMS

The Pelham bit is one of those enigmas that many horses seem to like and go kindly in but which human purists deplore as trying to do two jobs with one mouthpiece and doing neither very well. It looks very like a curb but has rings on the ends of the mouthpiece to take a pair of snaffle reins and also rings on the ends of the cheeks to take the curb reins. There are the usual hooks for the curb chain on the top rings of the upper branches of the cheeks and the little eyes for the lip strap.

The object of the Pelham is to give the horse only one mouthpiece to bother with and it is, I feel, certainly better for horses or ponies, and especially cobs, with small mouths. You can, of course, give both 'snaffle' and 'curb' aids with your two reins but it must be true that the single mouthpiece will transmit them less precisely than two bits would do. Perhaps it is this very fact that makes so many horses go so nicely and happily in a Pelham! Some people use

only one set of reins attached to a leather loop called a rounding which links both sets of rings. The action of this must be less precise than using two reins.

The mouthpiece on a Pelham is usually mullen-mouthed but you can buy ported Pelhams. You can also buy jointed Pelhams which really do seem to be pushing the boat out a bit as far as action and precision are concerned. They do allow tongue room but the curb aids must be very imprecise indeed because of the movability of the mouthpiece.

Another bit that belongs in the Pelham family is the **Kimblewick** which is used with only one pair of reins. It has a single mouthpiece, either mullen or ported, with D-shaped rings and chain hooks on eyes on the tops of them, or on little holes just below the eyes. The object is to use the bit mainly as a snaffle but then if extra leverage is needed, you are able to release your contact on the reins somewhat and lower your hands. The rein ends should then drop down the curved part of the bit ring. When you take up a contact again with your lowered hands, the reins, acting on the lower part of the bit ring, will pull back the straight part of the D-ring like the cheek of a curb bit, bringing the Kimblewick's curb chain into action – so that you get snaffle action and a bit of leverage as well.

Kimblewicks are used a fair amount in show jumping and for strong 'enthusiastic' horses who need a reminder to come to hand. They are also used on strong ponies whose small riders cannot manage two reins.

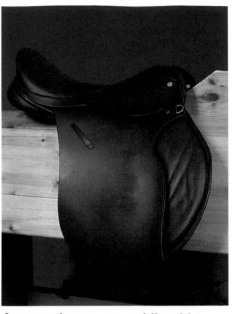

A modern, leather dressage saddle with a central, dipped seat, knee rolls and long girth straps.

A general purpose saddle with a central seat and knee rolls.

A jumping saddle with forward cut flaps to allow a shorter stirrup length and more acute knee bend.

An endurance riding saddle with padded seat, Ds for equipment attachment and a flap which allows for different stirrup lengths to relieve weight on the horse's back.

A cutback head (pommel) makes a saddle easier to fit on a horse with high, sharp withers.

A modern, synthetic saddle. (This one is a Wintec.)

Get someone to check there is a clear tunnel of daylight down the gullet of the saddle when the rider leans well forward – and therefore no pressure on the horse's spine.

Likewise check there is no pressure on the horse's spine when the rider leans backwards.

A show hack wearing a top quality leather double bridle with a decorative browband. The leatherwork is fine, without being flimsy, to show off the head.

A well-fitting snaffle bridle with a cavesson noseband (not rubbing the horse's facial bones) and an eggbutt snaffle bit adjusted at the right height in the horse's mouth and the right width. There is room for the ears but the throatlatch should be looser.

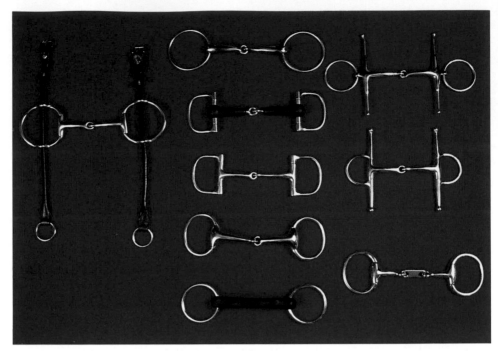

Snaffle bits. Left: Eggbutt gag snaffle. Middle row, from top: Wire-ring jointed snaffle, D-ring rubber-covered jointed snaffle, D-ring jointed snaffle, eggbutt jointed snaffle, straight-bar vulcanite loose-ring snaffle. Right, from top: Fulmer snaffle, cheek snaffle, Dr Bristol eggbutt snaffle.

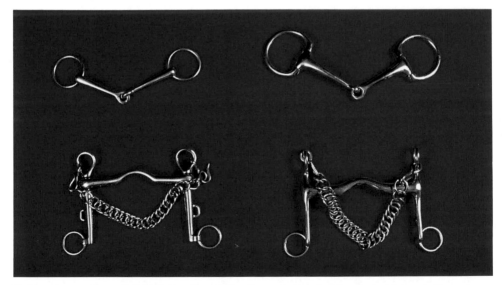

Bridoons and curb bits. On the left a loose-ring bridoon is shown above a sliding cheeked curb with a double-link chain. On the right is an eggbutt bridoon above a fixed-cheek curb and double-link chain. The combination on the right has thicker mouthpieces often used in dressage.

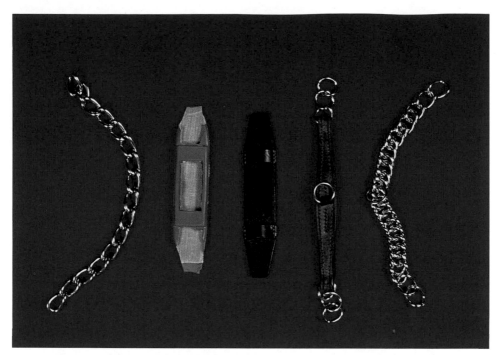

Curb chains and cover. From left: single-link chain, rubber cover, leather curb 'chain', double-link chain.

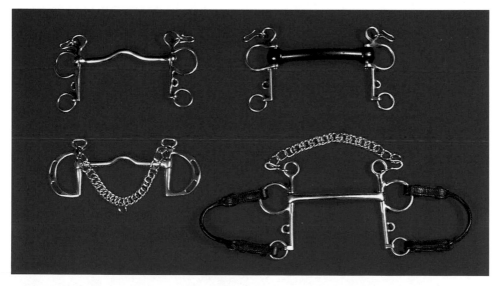

Pelhams and Kimblewick. Left, from top: A ported pelham, and below it, a Kimblewick, with eyes on the rings for a fixed rein attachment where a variable rein position is not wanted. Right, from top: a vulcanite mullen or half-moon pelham and a mullen-mouthed or half-moon pelham with roundings fitted so that a single rein can be used instead of two.

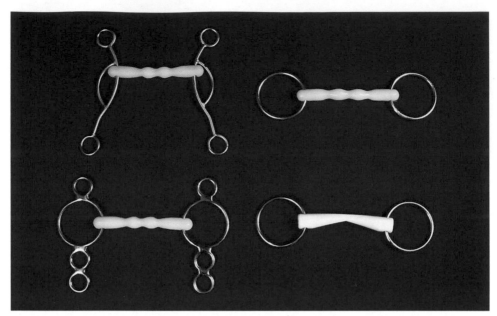

A selection of synthetic bits. Left, from top: an American gag above a three-ring snaffle which allows for a variable rein attachment. Right, from top: straight-bar loose-ring snaffle above a loose-ring snaffle with a mouthpiece shaped to allow room for the tongue.

The Schoolmasta rein.

Well-adjusted running reins fitted between the horse's forelegs. Fitted in this way, running reins are often called draw reins.

Running reins fitted under the saddle flap. This fitting is less severe than the fitting between the forelegs.

A horse equipped for lungeing, wearing a well-fitting lungeing cavesson with browband (the cheekpieces being well away from the eye). The trainer has the rein safely looped up off the ground (but not wrapped round his wrist which is extremely dangerous) and is carrying his lungeing whip behind him, pointing away from the horse. The horse also wears side-reins and a breastgirth attached to a roller. Ideally, he should be wearing a crupper to keep the roller back.

A horse ready for long-reining. The side-reins are optional, many trainers only using them for extra control with a difficult animal. The horse is dressed as for lungeing.

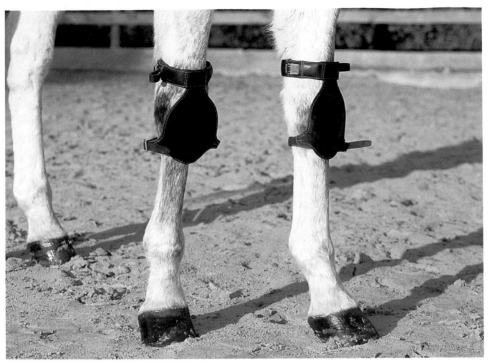

Above: Skeleton knee caps or knee pads, intended for use when exercising on roads or hard ground. The bottom straps should be much looser.

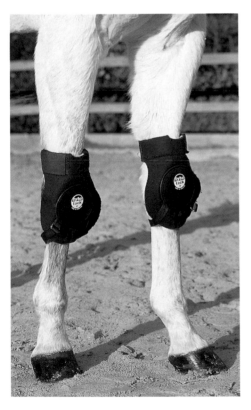

Left: Travelling knee pads.

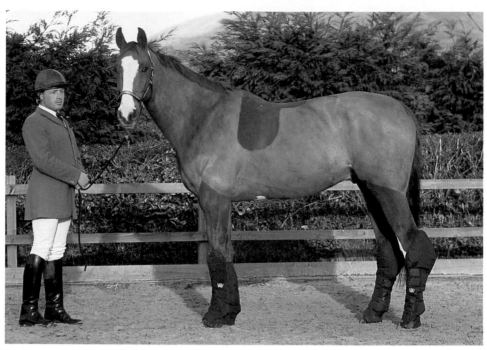

Full, modern, synthetic travelling boots on all four legs, protecting knees and hocks, right down the legs to the coronets.

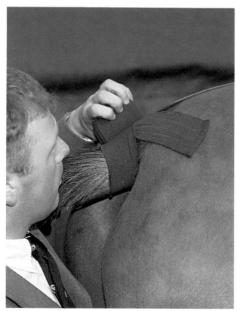

Putting on a tail bandage. Leave a flap of fabric as shown and take one turn round the root of the tail over it.

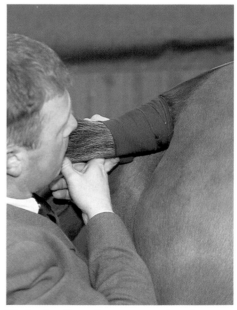

Turn the flap down over the dock and continue bandaging down over it.

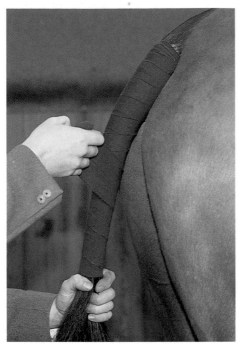

Bandage down almost to the end of the dock and back up again.

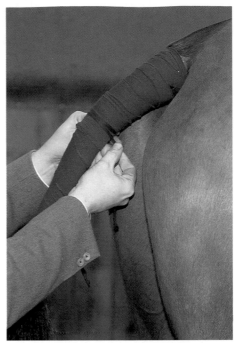

Tie the tapes no tighter than the bandage which should be firm but not tight. Make the bow at one side.

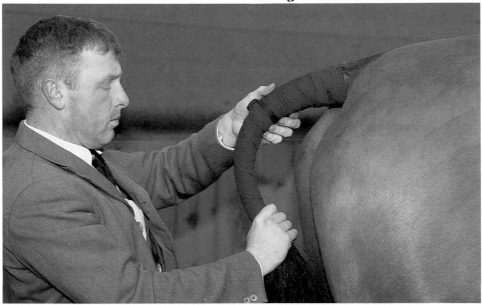

Bend the dock back into a comfortable position for the horse. Perhaps this is overdoing it a little!

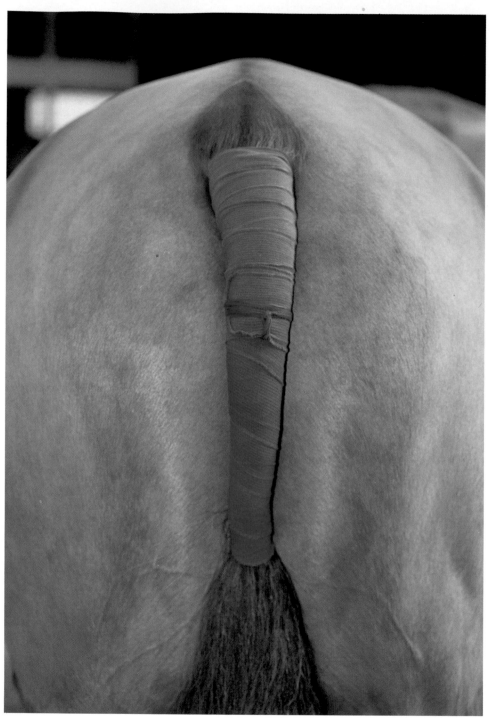

A neat job. Most people would prefer to fasten the bow more to the side of the tail, at least for travelling, so that the horse does not cause himself injury through pressure on the knot if he leans against the ramp.

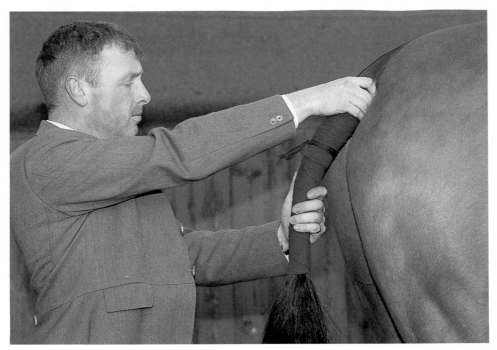

To remove a tail bandage, just grasp it right round the top of the dock ...

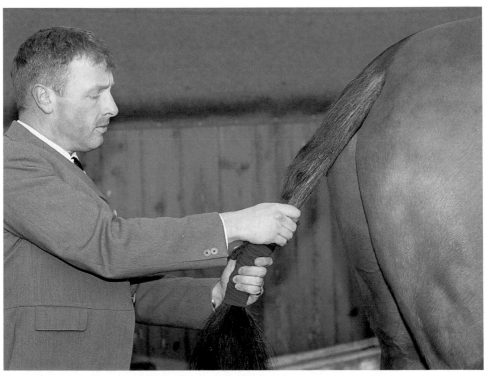

... and pull it down off the tail, unwinding and rolling it up later.

A synthetic, quilted stable rug with surcingles crossing under the belly. It fits well but could possibly come a little further up in the front round the base of the neck and more in front of the withers. These rugs are warm and comfortable for the horse and are easy to launder.

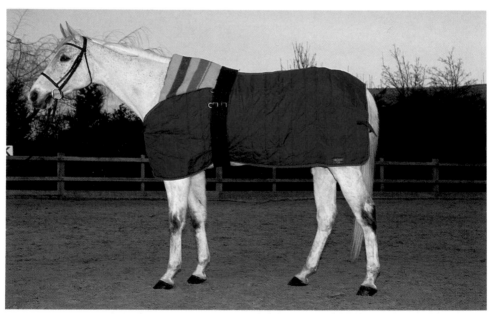

The old-fashioned way, albeit with a modern synthetic rug. This horse wears a rug with a Witney wool blanket underneath it and a roller securing the outfit. Obviously, this is nowhere near as comfortable for the horse as the crossing-surcingle style, particularly when the horse lies down.

A modern, Goretex turnout rug to which an old-fashioned surcingle has been added. This is uncomfortable for the horse and will stop the rug righting itself as a well-shaped rug will, when the horse moves or shakes.

A well-made, shaped, traditional New Zealand rug of canvas with hind leg straps. It comes well forward at the withers, over the tail and is deep enough to protect the belly. Such a rug should never have a surcingle added as it interferes with its function.

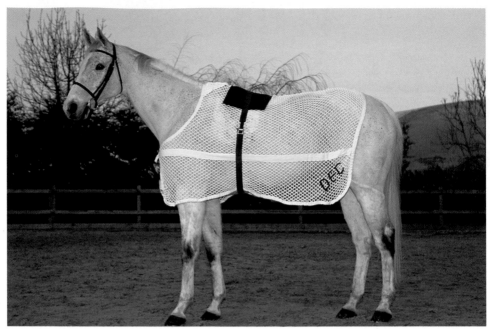

A mesh anti-sweat rug. Adding the surcingle and padding is certainly a safety measure when walking a horse in such a rug without a fillet string (which they usually do not have) but in practice they usually stay in place.

An exercise sheet or quarter rug folded under the saddle flaps to secure it, with the girth passing through the loops on its bottom edge. The fillet string round the back stops the rug blowing up, scaring the horse.

GAGS

The gag (strictly speaking a snaffle but generally placed in a group of its own) is another of those bits with pro and con factions. Because it tends to be used on horses who not only pull hard but also put their heads down to do so more effectively, it has a reputation of being severe and the horses who wear it are seen as tearaways. Both statements may be true but let us look a little more closely at what gags actually are.

As you will see from the illustration below, a gag snaffle has holes in the top and bottom of its rather large bit rings, through which run cords or occasionally rounded leathers (one through each ring). The cords have buckles at the top, which fasten in the usual way to the upper parts of the bridle cheekpieces, and rings at the lower ends for reins to fasten to. In addition, a pair of reins is fastened above the gag reins to the bit rings in the normal way so that the rider has two pairs of reins.

The idea is that you ride mostly in the usual way on the ordinary snaffle reins but if the horse gets his head too low for comfort or starts to take off with you into the next county, you can then use the gag reins. Pressure on these causes the bit rings to ride up the cords that run through them, raising the bit in the horse's mouth and creating a certain amount of downward pressure on the poll from the bridle headpiece.

It will be obvious to any intelligent reader that this bit must have a head-raising effect while the headpiece has a head-lowering one – contradictory, confusing and presumably ineffective, we may justifiably think – but in practice the gag does result in bringing the horse's head up, holding it in a salutary grip of sorts at both ends and bringing the horse under control. It works and few horses seem to resent it, particularly if you use it correctly and only put pressure on the gag reins when needed. Unfortunately, the gag is often seen used incorrectly, with only

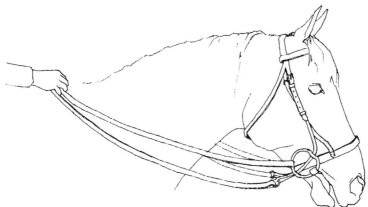

A correctly used gag snaffle. The rider rides mainly on the ordinary snaffle reins and may hold the gag rein under the little finger as shown, using it as required. Some riders hold the reins in different ways according to preference, but the main thing is to keep them separate so they can be used individually.

the gag rein, so that the gag effect is present more less all the time whenever the rider takes up a contact. This is not right at all and some horses ridden in this way may tend to respect their gags less and less.

BITLESS BRIDLES

Bitless bridles are not an odd way of riding a horse but are probably the oldest and, of course, a most effective one. There may be several reasons for riding a horse without a bit. He may have an injured mouth, a sore mouth due to teething or some mouth or dental operation; he may have a complete mental block where bits are concerned probably having suffered considerable pain and discomfort from a bit in the past; he may be one of those horses who is easy to hold and control without a bit but who becomes impossible with one. Or the matter may be rider orientated: perhaps the rider is a beginner, seems to have incurable 'mutton fists', or simply wishes to try a bitless bridle and see how the horse goes in one. Bitless bridles are also useful in disciplines where the horse is under saddle for long hours, when allowing him to snack en route or

---

Mouthpiece materials

We have discussed the various merits of stainless steel, nickel metals, copper and the newer, excellent metals coming onto the market but there are others which deserve consideration.

Perhaps the most common material, other than metal, is **vulcanite**, a hardened rubber that is softer than metal and which is usually seen in mullen-mouthed and straight-bar bits. It is liked by many horses but, as it is not as hard-wearing as metal, it has to be closely watched for wear.

Rubber is often used, both to cover the branches of jointed snaffles and to make mullen-mouthed snaffles, when it should have a strong nylon cord, rather than a metal chain, running through its centre for reinforcement. This fact should be stated on a label attached to the bit. The metal chain in poorer rubber snaffles can rot, break and leave you without a bit, as happened to Fred Winter riding Mandarin in the Prix d'Auteuil a generation or so ago – they still won this daunting French steeplechase! Rubber has a gentle, soft feel and many horses are happy with it, as with its harder relative, vulcanite.

Modern bits with improved nylon and plastic (and other) mouthpieces are now available and continue to be launched on an ever-fascinated, willing public! Fortunately, the ones currently available are a definite bonus to the 'bit world' and several international riders now use nothing else. The idea is that they are lightweight, gentle and non-threatening to the horse, and it is true that many horses seem to like them. They are also warmer than metal when first put in the mouth, as are rubber and vulcanite.

However, do be aware that there are still some cheap nylon bits on the market. These are of poor quality and, being easily roughened, can injure the horse's mouth.

during a break will be pleasanter and easier if he has no bit in his mouth. Whatever the reason, riding without a bit is quite feasible and popular – but which bridle to use?

The most commonly seen bridle is the incorrectly named 'hackamore', the correct name for which is the Blair pattern bitless or nose bridle. (A true hackamore is an item of Western riding quite unlike the Blair.) There is also the less-used and milder Scawbrig bridle, still effective and comfortable for the horse. Perhaps the two could be likened to the curb and snaffle of bitless bridles, respectively, as the Blair uses leverage and the Scawbrig direct tension.

The Blair pattern bridle

The Blair pattern bitless bridle is commonly seen in show jumping. The Blair has cheeks of varying lengths with eyes around the top for the noseband (a padded broad strap attached to the front eyes), the bottoms of the bridle cheekpieces and a curb strap (or, less commonly, chain) passing beneath the lower jaw in the curb or chin groove or just above it. When pressure is put on the reins, the cheeks are moved backwards from the bottom, the noseband receives a direct pull from the front eyes, the headpiece exerts downward pressure on the poll and the curb strap applies pressure in the chin groove. Therefore, pressure is felt by the horse all around the lower part of his head and on his poll. Individual use of each rein is also recognized by a schooled horse as an aid to turn to that particular side.

The longer the cheeks, the greater the leverage effect (the same applies

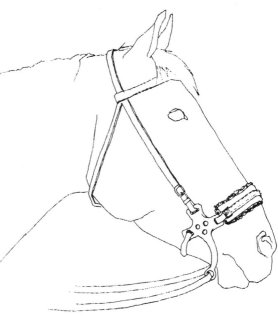

A Blair's pattern bitless bridle, which can exert a powerful leverage effect on the nose and behind the jaw.

to a curb bit) and the stronger the effect on the horse – the multiplying effect works here, too, of course. The Blair's pattern is, or can be, a 'strong' bridle and, in the wrong hands, severe bruising or even more serious injury could be caused. Used correctly and wisely, however, it is an effective bridle that seems to be here to stay.

The Scawbrig

Strictly speaking, the Scawbrig is intended to accustom a green or young horse to a bit but it can also be used for riding mature, schooled horses and gives quite enough control for all types of active riding and jumping (depending on the temperament of the horse), not just pottering about an enclosed *manège*.

It basically consists of a headpiece and cheekpieces and a front, padded, broad nose strap or band attached at each end to rings on the ends of the cheekpieces. There is also a second padded section (see illustration below) from the narrowed ends of which the reins are run through the rings on the ends of the cheekpieces. There is often a jowl strap to help to keep the bridle in place on the head (as well as the throatlatch) and which often runs through a loop on the top of the padded piece which goes under the jaw, again for stability and positioning.

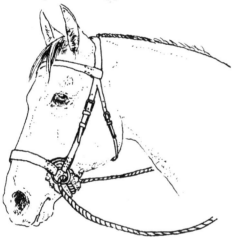

The Scawbrig bitless bridle is more direct and milder in action than the Blair, but still offers good control.

The Scawbrig operates on direct pressure, a pull on the reins tightening the two padded pieces round the whole of the lower part of the head (the nosebone and lower jaw). Even quite a hard pull or inadvertent jab from the reins will not upset most horses, hence its usefulness for beginners or clumsy riders. However, it should be stressed that the front section must be fitted on the nose bone *above* the nostrils to avoid any chance of the horse's breathing being interfered with, as horses cannot breath through their mouths to compensate for this.

As a training aid, the Scawbrig can have a separate headstall added for the attachment of a bit. Initially the bit can just hang, correctly positioned, in the horse's mouth with no reins attached while the rider continues to ride on the bitless reins. Once the horse has become used to the feel of a bit in his mouth and has learned to play with it, a pair of reins can be added to the bit and the rider can very gradually get the horse used to bit aids while still also using the bitless reins. Eventually, the bit takes over and the horse can go into an ordinary bridle.

There are other bitless bridles but these two are the most common and most useful.

NOSEBANDS

The noseband used with a bridle can have a devastating effect or no effect at all (including all points in between) on the horse, and can even alter the action of the bit.

The cavesson noseband
The simplest and probably the most common is the cavesson noseband, which is just a plain band of leather round the nose and jaw held up by leather straps. It serves no real purpose except to 'finish off' a horse's appearance, but is needed if a standing martingale is required (see Chapter 5). If it is fitted a little lower

than normal and fastened a little tighter, it can have a slight effect in discouraging the horse from opening his mouth to evade the bit.

The drop noseband

The drop or dropped noseband is less popular than it once was. It, too, consists of a headstall supporting the noseband itself, but in this noseband the front section is fitted a little lower than a cavesson and the rear section is fitted *below* the bit, passing along the chin groove and fastening on the near or left side below the lower lip. It is, therefore, the rear section that is dropped, and not so much the front. In any case, as with the Scawbrig, it is quite wrong, and can even be cruel and dangerous, to fit the front band so low that it presses on the nostrils and restricts the horse's breathing, even though this fitting is commonly seen among the unknowledgeable and even those who should know better.

The object of the drop noseband is to discourage, or prevent, the horse from opening his mouth to evade the action of the bit and it is effective in this. It also holds the ends of the bit mouthpiece snugly against the face and some horses do go better this way.

The flash noseband

The flash noseband is very popular these days. It consists of an ordinary cavesson with a thinner strap passing down from its centre in an upturned shape, passing below the bit, along the chin groove and fastening on the left in the same place as the drop noseband. Again its action is to discourage the horse from opening

A well-fitting eggbutt snaffle bridle with a correctly-adjusted drop noseband. It is set low enough to be effective without restricting the horse's breathing.

his mouth, at least too wide. It is not as effective as the drop noseband in this regard but many horses go better in it. It is also said to discourage the horse from crossing his jaw, but I feel no noseband can really do this as the horse can still cross his jaw within the confines of the pressure unless it is impossibly tight.

With the flash noseband you have the advantage that you have the mouth-closing effect plus the facility to attach a standing martingale, if you wish, without having to fit the horse with both a cavesson and a drop.

A well-fitting eggbutt snaffle bridle with a correctly adjusted flash noseband. The throatlatch, however, could be a little looser. There is plenty of ear room and the noseband is not so high that it will rub underneath the sharp facial bones. It is roomy enough to allow a finger to slide under it easily.

A well-fitting eggbutt snaffle bridle with a Grakle noseband. These nosebands are usually more comfortable and effective if they have a little loop linking the straps under the jaw.

The Grakle noseband

The Grakle noseband was named after a Grand National winner who wore one. It consists of thinnish straps crossing over the front of the horse's face, usually with a little pad of sheepskin or felt under the cross to prevent pressure and rubbing.

As with all types of noseband, the top straps pass under the bridle cheekpieces, above the bit and then fasten below the jaw, while the bottom pieces pass under the bit, pass along the chin groove and fasten on the left.

The purpose of the Grakle is to discourage the horse from opening his mouth and crossing his jaw. If he does try to open his mouth he will feel pressure on the front of his nose, which will discourage him and also has the psychological effect of steadying him down somewhat.

To help to stabilize the noseband and stop the upper branches sliding up too much, there should be a short, vertical piece or loop of leather resting in the groove between the two lower branches of the horse's jaw, linking top and bottom straps together.

These are the most useful and commonly seen nosebands in current use.

REINS

It is most important that your reins are comfortable in your hands as otherwise you will find it difficult to give good aids. A good general width seems to be 7/8 in for ladies and about 2.5cm (1in) for men, but you can get narrower and wider reins than this. Double and Pelham bridles have the curb reins narrower than the bridoon reins so that the rider can easily differentiate between them by feel. For the same reason it is useful to have the gag reins narrower than the snaffle reins on a gag bridle.

Plain leather reins are used on double and Pelham bridles and can also be used on snaffle bridles. They have the disadvantage of becoming quite slippery when wet with rain or sweat. **Rubber-covered** reins prevent this, being covered with pimpled rubber that can be replaced (usually once only as the stitching weakens the leather) when worn. They also give a good grip for horses who take hold. **Laced** leather reins have little strips of leather set down their hand-parts in a herringbone pattern, again with the object of giving greater grip, particularly when wet, and **plaited** leather reins have the same effect but stretch quite badly in use. It is possible to get **webbing** reins with little strips of leather set horizontally across the handparts for grip, but both with these and laced leather many people find the added strips irritating. You can get plaited **cotton** reins made to order and these are excellent, providing absorbency and softness. This means that they are kind on your hands and are not slippery when wet.

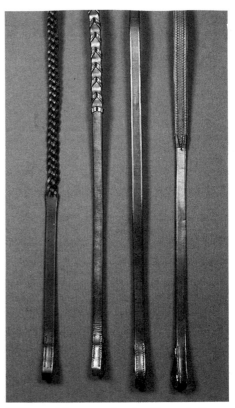

Different types of rein. From left: plaited, laced, plain, rubber-covered.

Length can be important. Normally you want the reins to be long enough to leave a reasonable loop hanging down the horse's offside (right) shoulder when you have taken up a contact in walk, a drop of about 30cm (1ft) being usual. You can buy shorter reins for show jumping. The extra length is useful as it allows you to knot or bridge your reins when jumping or riding a horse that has a habit of throwing his head down and sending you flying off over his head, or when riding a puller, as you can rest the bridge against the lower part of his neck when the going gets tough and he ends up pulling against himself while you save your strength and have a breather! Similarly, when riding a bucker, the bridge can prevent you from being lurched forward and off.

Conversely, if your reins are too long, the extra length can end up wrapping itself round your right foot – not exactly a safe practice!

Fastenings

The most common way of attaching reins to bits is by means of hook studs. A hook stud is a metal hook set onto the rein by means of a separate piece of leather a short way down from the end. The end of the rein passes through the bit ring and back through a leather keeper. There is a slit in the rein which you press down over the hook and pull

backwards to secure it and the tip of the rein then passes through a second keeper. From the 'outside' the fastening looks neat as the hook stud is on the inside of the rein. Hook studs are also used at the ends of the cheekpieces for fastening round the bit.

Stitched-in bits are rare these days and quite impractical, although undeniably the neatest fastening you can get. There are also loop fastenings, where the reins simply pass through the bit rings and back through loops on their ends. Although fairly secure, loops are not as strong as hook studs. Finally there are buckle fastenings, generally regarded as ugly and 'down market', although used almost exclusively on police and military bridles.

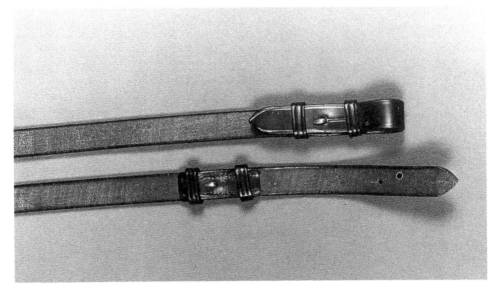

A hook stud fastening, the most common method of attachment in modern bridles. As shown by the top rein the hook stud is undone and the hole and slit in the end can be seen. To fasten it (below), the end is doubled up through the keepers, the slit pressed down over the hook and the end pulled down firmly till the hook protrudes through and is held by the hole, making a secure fastening.

Reins fasten with a small buckle and keeper at the 'hand' end which prevents a rein trailing dangerously should you drop one. This is only undone for cleaning purposes or for passing through the rings on a running martingale.

Materials

All high-quality bridlework is made of leather, some of it very fine for showing off elegant heads in the showring, wider and more utilitarian for daily work, or even wider for disguising a large, ugly head (fine leatherwork shows off a fine head but would accentuate a large, ugly one, whereas broad leather would swamp a small head).

It is generally considered good taste to have fairly plain bridles, except in Western circles, but plaited or stitched and padded nosebands and browbands are common, particularly in showing, and do look good. Coloured browbands in various patterns, usually of velvet, are used on children's ponies and hacks and browbands with metal inserts are common in dressage and show jumping and can look very attractive.

Synthetic (usually some sort of plastic) materials are now being used quite widely and seem to be popular and practical, especially in endurance riding circles. Nylon webbing is still available but many feel that it looks cheap and nylon can certainly be rough on a horse's skin and the rider's hands. The problem with much synthetic bridlework is that the buckles are of poor quality and rust easily, so if you do want some sort of easily cleaned, synthetic

tack, try to get good quality buckles.

Some people find it practical to use synthetic tack for everyday wear and to keep their good leather tack for 'best'.

Types of bridles and bits

Snaffle

∪ single jointed – works on bars and lips. eggbutt – avoids pinching of lips loose or wire ring – allows more movement of the bit
∪ double jointed – works on bars, lips and tongue – the French snaffle is a mild bit – the Doctor Bristol is a severe bit
∪ mullen-mouth or half-moon – mild – often made of rubber or vulcanite, works on tongue and bars
∪ straight bar – sometimes made of vulcanite, works on tongue and bars

Double

∪ with curb (Weymouth) bit (straight, ported or mullen-mouthed) and jointed snaffle (bridoon) bit, also curb chain – for horses that have achieved a degree of collection who already go well in a snaffle bit – two reins – works on poll, chin groove, tongue, lips and bars

Pelham

∪ one bit fulfilling two functions, two reins or one rein on leather roundings – usually a mullen-mouthed bit, less often ported or jointed – works on poll, chin groove, tongue, lips and bars

Kimblewick

∪ a mullen-mouthed or ported bit and one rein – good on children's ponies that pull

Curb chains for use with curb, Pelham and Kimblewick bits

∪ metal – single link – severe
– flat link – flatter and more comfortable
– double link – most comfortable of the three

∪ leather – comfortable and recommended

∪ elastic – less comfortable and less precise as an aid

∪ felt-backed leather – comfortable and recommended

Gag

∪ really a snaffle bit – used with two reins, one acting as a snaffle rein, the other running through a special gag ring – acts on the poll, tongue, bars and lips – for strong pullers and horses who put their heads down to evade the bit

Bitless bridle

∪ acts on front of nose and chin groove – for horses with mouth injuries or who dislike bits
Blair pattern bridle – acts on poll, chin groove and nose – one rein
Scawbrig bridle – acts on nose and lower jaw – one rein

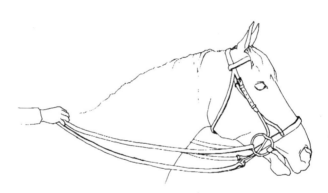

CHAPTER 5

SCHOOLING ACCESSORIES

Unfortunately, as this is an imperfect world, what should really be regarded as schooling or training aids are sometimes needed permanently on certain animals. The things we ask horses to do are hard work for them physically and, on an individual basis, their conformation may not be ideally suited to the particular move-ment or way of going we are asking for. Also, the rider may not be too brilliant either and may hinder the horse in his efforts to comply with their requests. This may mean that he goes 'wrongly' in an effort to go at all and we may resort to some piece of equipment to get them to go 'correctly'. It can be a vicious circle but schooling aids do have their place for all horses, provided we understand what is happening when we use them, only use them when they are really needed and only permanently as a last resort.

MARTINGALES

Martingales are a good example of a training aid that often ends up as a permanent part of a particular horse or pony's equipment when he is tacked up. There are two main kinds of martingale in use although you will also see variations of them.

Running martingale
Probably the least harmful and most useful is the running martingale. It has a neckstrap round the base of the neck with a strap passing down between the forelegs and fastening around the girth at the breastbone. This same strap also divides upwards in two branches ending in metal rings, one rein passing through each ring. (The neckstrap is there simply to support the strap and stop it from looping down dangerously near the forelegs which could otherwise become entangled in it, although the neckstrap can also be used to steady the rider, like a proper neckstrap.)

The rings are free to 'run' along each rein, hence its name. Its purpose is to give the horse a steadier feel on the bit in his mouth should he throw his head about. Also, should he raise it above a desirable level, or should the rider raise his or her hands too high, the rings keep the reins down and keep the action of the bit on the bars instead of the corners of the lips. This martingale is obviously useful for novice horses and riders who may be inclined to throw their heads and hands about and who have not yet learned to keep a steady headcarriage and a steady, communicative contact on the bit, respectively.

It is fitted so that when the straps (when not on the reins) are held diagonally up the shoulder they more or less reach the withers; then, when the reins are passed through their rings, the latter should be at the right height so that they only exert pressure on the reins when the head or hands are raised too much.

Rein stops, little stiff loops of leather or rubber, are fitted to each rein between the rings and the bit ends of the reins to stop the rings being caught on the bit or on the horse's teeth should he have the habit, as some young horses do, of catching hold of the reins. A tight rubber loop called a martingale stop is fitted at the point where the branching strap passes through the neckstrap at the horse's breast, to stop it looping down between the forelegs.

The standing martingale

The standing martingale is also meant to combat the effects of a horse raising his head above a desirable point but acts in a different way. Again, there is a neckstrap and a strap passing to the girth, but this strap continues upwards in a single strap and fastens to the back of a cavesson or the cavesson part of a flash noseband. It is fitted so that when it is fastened in place you can lift the strap so that it almost touches the underside of the horse's throat (where the throatlatch goes). At this length, when the horse raises his head too much, the strap will pull on the back of the noseband, very effectively keeping the head down.

Obviously, no rein stops are needed with a standing martingale, but a martingale stop should be used.

A running martingale correctly adjusted, with the rings just about to come into effect should the horse raise his head higher than this.

The problem with standing martingales is that if they are fitted just slightly too tight, horses can all too easily learn to lean on them via the noseband. This not only makes for a lazy way of going but also one which develops the wrong muscles in the neck and forehand and, ultimately, makes going correctly even more difficult for the horse. When the martingale is removed, one can see some very strange performances indeed as the confused horse tries to keep his balance without being able to lean on his noseband!

Standing martingales must never be fitted to the back strap of a drop noseband even if the noseband's front strap is fitted correctly (a little lower than a cavesson) as this can interfere with the horse's breathing and is also too severe in its action. One fitting that can most definitely be regarded as cruel is to fit the standing martingale to a little coupling which joins the two bit rings so that the martingale actually operates on the bit.

The Irish martingale

The Irish martingale is simply a short strip of leather with a ring at each end through which the reins pass, the martingale itself lying on the reins under the horse's neck. Rein stops are needed with this. Its purpose is simply to keep the reins down and together in horses that have the habit of throwing their heads around and getting a rein over their heads, which virtually puts them out of control.

TRAINING REINS

Under this heading we may group the Market Harborough rein (often

A helper checking the fit of a standing martingale by pressing the strap up into the horse's gullet.

called a martingale), draw reins, running reins, the Chambon and the de Gogue and two fairly new patented aids, the Schoolmasta and the Equi-Weight.

The Market Harborough

The Market Harborough, like the two martingales described above, consists of a neckstrap and a strap going down to the girth at the lower end. At the upper end it divides into two straps (or has two clip-on reins) which are longer than those of a running martingale. Each passes through one side of the bit ring, then comes back to clip onto one of four pairs of spaced-out metal Ds sewn onto ordinary, or specially made, reins. Sometimes they buckle onto these reins, although this is less common.

The purpose of the Market Harborough is similar to that of a running martingale and many people prefer it. It is adjusted so that when the horse raises his head above a desired level, the contact is transferred to the Market Harborough, rather than to the reins, which exerts a downward pressure similar to the feel of a running martingale in the horse's mouth. The looser it is fitted, the less is its effect, and vice versa; if fitted to the pairs of Ds nearest the rider's hands, its effect can be severe. Wisely used, however, it can be very useful.

Draw reins

Draw reins and running reins are often confused even by experts, partly because there are two fittings for the latter, both of which are correctly called running reins!

Draw reins are, in fact, one continuous rein which goes over the poll, down the sides of the head, through the bit rings to the rider's hands. They have a similar effect on the horse to a gag snaffle in that they

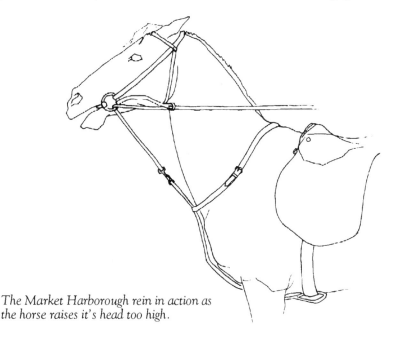

The Market Harborough rein in action as the horse raises it's head too high.

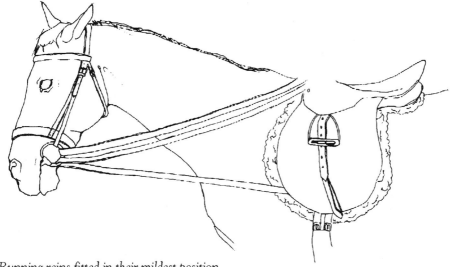

Running reins fitted in their mildest position.

raise the bit in the mouth to encourage him to bring his head up yet exert a downward influence on the poll. However, the bit 'feel' predominates and draw reins effectively discourage horses from getting their heads too low (maybe down between their knees to help them buck you off!). They are also good for horses who have learned to lean on the bit or to pull.

The rider rides on ordinary reins, only using the draw rein when needed. The draw rein can be positioned in the hand as a curb rein, for clarity.

Running reins
As mentioned, running reins can be fitted in two ways. The mildest way is to fit them running from the rider's hands through the bit rings and back, fastening round the girth or girth tabs under the saddle flaps on each side. A more severe fitting is to have the reins returning from the bit rings between the forelegs and fastening round the girth as for a martingale. Both fittings encourage the horse to lower his head and bring in his nose, so they are used for horses who poke their noses, raise their heads, lean, etc.

Again, the rider should ride on ordinary reins, only using the running reins when needed.

The Chambon
Unlike the aids we have discussed so far, the Chambon (pronounced 'shombon') is not used when riding but when lungeing or loose schooling to persuade the horse to lower his head and neck. Some experts use it as a matter of course when lungeing, to teach the horse more quickly that it is easier and more comfortable for him to go with his head and neck down and 'stretched' in a relaxed way as this frees the hindquarters (so the theory goes) and encourages the back to swing. The horse can bring his hind legs well under him and all this encourages him to go 'from the

The Chambon is an excellent training aid if carefully used. The horse is also wearing a lunge-ing cavesson, bridle with bit, roller, breastgirth, crupper and, on his forelegs, brushing and over-reach boots with fetlock boots on his hind legs.

back end forwards' right from the early stages of schooling. This position makes for correct muscular development, making it easier for the horse to bear weight after being backed and, it is hoped, instilling in him the correct way of going and making it less likely that, given a good rider, he will start hollowing his back under weight and poking his nose to counteract it, both of which make for an inefficient way of going. Of course, a poor rider will encourage him to go badly anyway.

The Chambon consists of a padded poll strap with a small pulley wheel on each end. A cord clips to each bit ring and passes up the sides of the face and over the pulley, then down to the breast where the cords fasten to two short pieces of leather on a strap that passes through the forelegs and fastens, in the usual way, round a roller .

When the horse raises his head above the level desired by his trainer (which should be carefully assessed according to the horse's conforma-tion and natural way of going), the poll strap exerts downward pressure on the poll and the bit is drawn upwards (but not backwards as, for example, with a gag or draw reins). It may confuse readers to be told that this encourages the horse to *lower* his head, having read that gags and draw reins have a head-*raising* effect, but in practice this is what happens! It seems that the horse realizes that this uncomfortable feeling only occurs when he raises his head, so he lowers it to relieve the discomfort. Not being quite as stupid as some imagine, horses also soon seem to catch on to the fact that they operate the Chambon themselves – unlike other devices, the pressure on poll and mouth is directly related to the height at which they carry their heads. The only control the trainer has over the Chambon is when he or she is initially adjusting it.

The de Gogue

The de Gogue rein can be used when lungeing or loose schooling and also when riding. One fitting, the independent fitting, is again operated by the horse after initial adjustment by the trainer or rider, while another, the command fitting, is operated by the rider.

In the *independent* mode, a strap is fastened round the girth or roller at the breastbone, then passes up between the forelegs, ending at the breast in two short pieces of leather that form a small fork with rings or Ds on their ends. Cords clip onto these rings, each one passing up the side of the poll where they run, as with the Chambon, through a ring or pulley on each end of a padded poll strap, down through each bit ring and back to clip onto the breast straps.

Obviously, the rider or trainer has no control over the de Gogue used in this way; the horse operates it himself, giving himself a similar uncomfortable feel to the Chambon when he raises his head too high.

When used in the *command* mode, after passing through the bit rings the cords clip onto special short reins in the rider's hands so that the rider has direct control of their effect. Again, there is an ordinary pair of reins which should be used most of the time, the de Gogue only coming into use when needed.

The Schoolmasta

The Schoolmasta rein consists of a cotton numnah with a small pulley wheel on each side of the pommel or

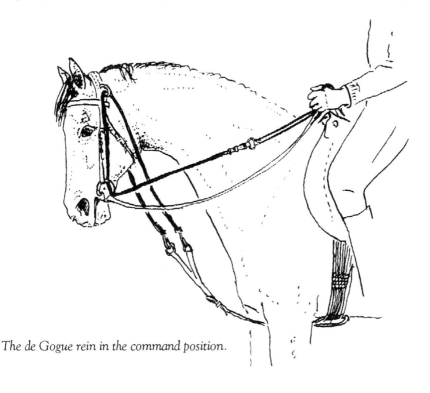

The de Gogue rein in the command position.

wither area. A cord runs through these and attaches to reins fastened to each bit ring. The rider does not use the Schoolmasta rein but rides on normal reins, so this is another aid that the horse operates himself.

The rein is intended for hard-pulling horses, those that lean and are heavy in the hand or who poke their noses. The rein is adjusted so that it has no effect until the horse starts to indulge in any of the above activities: he then soon realizes, apparently, that he is only pulling against himself, that this is uncomfortable, and stops doing whatever it is he is doing. The advantage is that the rider does not have to cope with the horse's antics but is able to maintain a balanced position in the saddle and, most important, a light, giving contact on the ordinary rein which the horse also seems to realize is coming from the rider and not from his own efforts to pull against the Schoolmasta rein. In practice, it does seem to work well and is also available in a design for use on the unridden horse, being attached to a roller in that case.

The Equi-Weight

The Equi-Weight, like most new devices in the horse world, has come in for a good deal of adverse criticism, but it is one of those inventions that really seems to work in a beneficial way in practice. It takes the form of a solid cylindrical weight clipped to both bit rings, worn by the horse behind his chin (three weights are available for different sizes and types of horse or pony). It is used during lungeing, long-reining or loose schooling and, once fitted, is not under the control of the trainer but of the horse, who adjusts his way of going and head and neck carriage so that the weight is comfortable to carry when his head and neck are in the correct position and he is using his body well.

Although a weight carried directly on the bit may seem to go against the principles of lightness in riding, the weight is claimed to teach lightness and acceptance of the bit, as well as developing the horse's action, physique and topline. Should he try to lean on the weight, as he might on a rider's contact, he soon finds there is nothing to lean on: to keep his balance he has to bring his hind legs further underneath his body, lowering his quarters, rounding his back and going from the 'back end' in the correct way. In addition, he learns that by carrying his head and neck in a fairly low, rounded position, he actually relieves himself of the weight in his mouth, the weight then being directly transferred to his poll via the bridle cheekpieces and headpiece, which itself encourages a lowish, relaxed head and neck carriage. Getting the horse to go in this way during early schooling, before backing and just afterwards, brings him on physically and mentally without, initially, having to cope with the weight of a rider. He also has no possibly erratic hand contact to worry about and so learns to trust the bit and not evade it.

ROLLERS

A roller is simply a broad, substantial belt passing round the horse's ribcage behind his withers and elbows, preferably in the horse's natural girth groove if he has one – not all do. A roller is used during schooling to attach side-reins (see Chapter 6) when lungeing or long-reining and also helps to accustom the horse to the feel of something round his girth in preparation for being saddled up and backed.

The roller will have various Ds and rings on it to permit different levels and methods of fastening side-reins, according to the trainer's requirements, for long reins to pass through and also to attach a crupper and breastgirth.

The roller should have the last two items mentioned attached to it to help keep it in its proper position. The crupper keeps it back and prevents it creeping forward and digging into the muscles behind the shoulders, irritating the horse and encouraging him to shorten his action in self-defence, whereas the breastgirth helps to stop it sliding back which it may do depending on the horse's conformation or condition. Like many items of tack these days, rollers are available in leather, natural fabric (usually woollen webbing) or synthetic materials.

Some trainers manage very well without a roller and attach side-reins and other devices to the saddle, either to the Ds on the pommel, round the girth or girth tabs under the flap or round the girth between the forelegs. However, most people prefer a proper roller where possible.

PROS AND CONS OF 'GADGETS'

Purists nearly always condemn out of hand anything that smacks of gadgetry, as certain schooling accessories or aids are often called. They accuse them of being 'short cuts' in training, of developing the horse physically before he is mentally mature, of side-stepping the correct, classical methods of long, slow schooling, and similar charges. The facts are that many experts use them as an aid in getting through to the horse and as a way of getting him to understand what is wanted more effectively and quickly than months of schooling without them may do. Used wisely, skillfully and with sympathy and understanding, there is nothing wrong with gadgets of any kind if they do the job without hurting or frightening the horse.

They are usually very much a means to an end but, as mentioned at the beginning of this chapter, there are cases where some, such as martingales, need to be used indefinitely and/or permanently. If this enables a horse or pony to do a useful job more comfortably and safely, surely there is nothing wrong with this either, especially when the alternative might be an animal that no one wants or can handle and whose only destiny is death.

CHAPTER 6

LUNGEING AND LONG-REINING EQUIPMENT

Lungeing and long-reining are two valuable techniques for the early schooling of the horse and pony, and they require specific equipment if they are to be carried out effectively and safely. In neither technique (with a few exceptions) does the horse have a rider; in addition he is 'green' (uneducated) in the early stages (although with long-reining it is possible to bring a horse to a very high standard of schooling indeed) and untrained, unridden horses can be hard to control. It is important, therefore, that the correct equipment is properly fitted and used so that the procedures can be carried out as effectively and safely as possible.

CAVESSONS

Lungeing cavessons are standard equipment for both procedures, although bridles are often used as training advances, with or without a cavesson in addition.

A lungeing cavesson is similar to a headcollar but fits more closely and has a padded nosepiece to which are attached rings for the connection of

the lunge rein or long reins. There will be a ring on the front, where the lunge rein is normally fastened, and rings at the sides, either in front of or behind the cheekpieces, for long reins (the positioning of the reins depending on the trainer's school of thought).

The object of the cavesson is to provide firm, steady attachment for the rein/s and to this end it must fit well, must not pull round or twist on the horse's head in use, rub his eye or any other part, or in any way irritate him. Should a young or difficult horse get up to antics during work, the cavesson must remain secure and not be able to be rubbed off by the horse or pulled off or out of position by the trainer via the reins.

In addition to the padded nosepiece, cavessons have a headpiece adjusted by a buckle on the nearside. The nosepiece has a strap continuing round the back (with a buckle) and there is an adjustable jowl strap. The whole thing is fitted snugly, but not tightly, to the head. The best cavessons have a browband for extra stability and to prevent any chance of the headpiece slipping down the neck, and cheekpieces that are set a little further back than normal to prevent rubbing the eye, with diagonally set straps between them and the nosepiece, again for stability.

Cavessons can be made of leather (the best, strongest and most stable) or various synthetic materials. In my view, the nylon web ones are not steady or sturdy enough for the job and easily slide round no matter how tightly they are fitted.

Lungeing or long-reining equipment
∪ lunge line – 10.5m (35ft)
∪ long reins – 10.5m (35ft), finer than
   lunge line
∪ lunge whip
∪ roller with crupper and breastplate
∪ lunge cavesson
∪ side-reins
∪ brushing boots – worn all round
∪ over-reach boots – worn on forefeet

LUNGEING AND LONG-REINING EQUIPMENT

Lungeing reins are normally made of tubular cotton webbing with a loop at the hand end and a buckle on a swivel fitting at the other end, which normally attaches to the centre-front ring on the cavesson. The rein is usually up to about 10.5m (35ft) long but the trainer, by looping the rein in his or her hand (*never* round the wrist in case of being dragged), can lengthen and shorten the rein at will – the shorter the rein, the smaller and more difficult the circle becomes for the horse.

For long-reining, most trainers prefer a lighter-weight, probably synthetic, rein although these can be difficult to get and many people make do with two lungeing reins.

Some trainers do not use anything else, but most prefer to do the job with the horse also wearing a roller, fitted with a breastgirth and crupper, so that **side-reins** can be fitted. These run from the side rings of the cavesson (or the bit rings if a bridle, minus reins and noseband, is used as well) to the Ds or rings on the roller, the lower fittings used for younger horses and the higher ones for those that are more advanced and have achieved a certain level of muscular development and a higher, more educated head carriage. They can also be fitted to a saddle, in the absence of a roller, round the girth.

The purpose of side-reins is partly psychological, as the horse then feels more under control. They give the horse a preliminary idea of rein contact and teach him to flex his jaw and poll, to some extent, to the bit: they are not meant to fix the horse's head in a certain position although they do discourage the horse from tossing his head around.

Some trainers like side-reins with rubber rings in them to give a feel of flexibility to the contact; others maintain that the plain ones are best as the horse gets instant relief when he gives to the bit. This does not happen when side-reins with rubber rings are fitted at all tightly, as the rings simply take up any slack created by the horse.

If side-reins are fitted at all tightly, they can actually encourage the horse to lean on and/or evade the bit and can make his neck ache, causing him to go in all sorts of peculiar ways to relieve this.

Side-reins are straps with buckles for easy adjustment at the end that fastens to the roller (trigger clips are also used) and clips at the ends fastening to the bit rings or cavesson rings.

A **lungeing whip** is a necessary item of equipment which can be surprisingly difficult to handle and balance at first. As lightweight a whip as possible is advisable for ease of use, and the trainer should practise flicking out the long thong to just touch inanimate objects first before being let loose on a live animal with it! The idea is *not* to crack it like a circus whip, nor to sting or cut the horse with it: it is meant more as a visual guide to the horse than anything else and forms part of the trainer's body language, to which horses are very alert and receptive. When the whip is pointed in front of the horse or at his shoulder, he should learn to slow or stop, and to go or speed up when it is pointed at his hip or hindquarters. However, a tactful flick on any part of the horse can be used by a skilled trainer to reinforce verbal requests.

CHAPTER 7

HEADCOLLARS AND HALTERS

Headcollars give basic control when leading or tying up a well-behaved horse or pony. They are like a substantial bridle or a lungeing cavesson without the padded nosepiece and rings. There are various sorts and they are available in leather (either vegetable-tanned or chrome-tanned which gives a pale green colour, the chrome tanning causing leather to stretch more than vegetable-tanned leather before breaking), nylon webbing which is very common and, in my view, quite abhorrent as well as being a safety risk, and various other synthetic materials.

Top-quality headcollars are of stout, vegetable-tanned leather and are called **Albert** headcollars. They have double-thickness cheekpieces with three rows of stitching, a rolled leather throatlatch and solid brass buckles and other fittings. A brass nameplate can be fitted down the nearside cheekpiece with the horse's name engraved on it.

The best headcollars are adjustable not only by means of a buckle on the end of the cheekpiece but also on the throatlatch and nosepiece, too, to get a really snug, safe yet comfortable fit. Many headcollars have nosebands that are much too big and people fasten them too high

to compensate for this so that they rub underneath the horse's sharp facial bones. The noseband should just allow the horse to move his jaws comfortably when eating (as they are often worn in the field and stable although this is not desirable), and the noseband should come midway between the ends of the sharp face bones and the corners of the lips. The best headcollars also have a browband to prevent the common happening of the headpiece sliding down the neck and creating an uncomfortable pull on the nose. The throatlatch should obviously be fitted just tightly enough to prevent the horse rubbing the headcollar off and getting free.

Everyday headcollars can be of leather, stitched and/or riveted together, adjustable only at the headpiece. Field headcollars are often of chrome-tanned leather with non-brass, metal fittings (stainless steel, as ever, being best and rustless). Nylon web headcollars are extremely strong and will rarely break should the horse get caught up in the field, leading to accidents and injury. They also fray with use and can easily catch on things. Leather does not fray and will break under pressure from a horse that is caught up and panicking.

An excellent type of headcollar with browband, permitting full adjustment. It allows plenty of room for the ears and fits closely yet will still allow the horse to move his jaws in comfort when eating.

A webbing halter on a heavy horse foal. Note the special knot to prevent it tightening on the head.

The fittings on a headcollar consist of the buckle/s and of rings joining the leather straps, with either a ring or a square-shaped D at the bottom under the jaw for the attachment of a leadrope or rack (tying-up) chain for horses kept in stalls, although strong ropes can be used for these, too. Thankfully, this method of securing horses is going out of fashion, although it is still widely used in police and military stables.

HALTERS

Halters are made of rope or cotton webbing. They are not as convenient as headcollars as the leadrope is part of them and cannot be detached. They are purely for leading or tying

up animals, but they have to be tied in a special way (see the illustration above right) to prevent them pulling tight on the head or coming undone and falling off. They are not widely used apart from in the heavy-horse world.

LEADROPES

Most people feel that the most widely available leadropes are too weak these days. Twisted cotton is extremely common and not very strong or hardwearing. The older jute ropes are much better but have to be hunted for.

Leadropes should be about 2m long (over 6ft) to be useful but many are shorter. They have either spring or trigger clips on the ends for attachment to the headcollar bottom D, but some have a simple bound loop through which the other end of the rope is threaded after passing through the D. This is less convenient but is safer than any clip, both types of which have been known to injure horses.

Showing leadreins are of leather, whitened cotton webbing or a combination of the two, sometimes with a length of brass chain at the 'horse' end. The idea is that they look of better quality and smarter than leadropes.

SHOWING HEADSTALLS

An Arab showing headstall. Some also have throatlatches.

There is a variety of headcollars or headstalls for showing various categories of horse or pony. Most showing headstalls consist of a smart headcollar, usually made of leather, perhaps with a decorative browband and bosses or rosettes at the ends, or else plain metal discs. Some can have small loops or bit attachments that clip to the side Ds to take a bit for showing your stock. Arab headstalls are usually of very fine (sometimes too fine and therefore weak) rolled leather to show off Arabs' fine heads, and may also have a chain section passing under the jaw to which a leadrein is clipped (see illustration above).

Although you could use showing headstalls for everyday use, many are expensive and it seems rather foolish. Some, too, are weaker than sturdy, everyday types: this in itself is foolish as if an animal is going to play up it will surely do so in the strange and exciting atmosphere of a showground where you will need extra strength and control, not less.

There is nothing wrong with showing an animal in hand in a well-cleaned and polished ordinary head-collar, particularly the Albert type, with polished metal, preferably brass, fittings, although some categories of animal, such as stallions and broodmares, are shown in bridles, the former in stallion show bridles with brass fittings and decorative bit cheeks, and the latter in ordinary double bridles with long reins to allow for leading. Animals of two years (often three) and under are not normally shown bitted, or, if they are, the bit is usually free in the mouth with no direct contact to the hand, or they are led by means of a coupling which puts more stress on the noseband than on the bit, to avoid spoiling a young, uneducated mouth.

CHAPTER 8

LEG PROTECTION

Apart from feeding, the subject of horses' legs probably evokes more discussion among horse people than anything else! The horse's legs are very vulnerable to injury and there is much misunderstanding over what we can do to protect against those injuries. Impossible claims are made for ordinary bandages (for example, conventionally applied exercise bandages do *not* support the leg), while bandages or boots, if wrongly applied, can actually do a good deal of harm to the leg.

Most of the items available protect the horse against knocks and bangs but not from the over-stress often experienced during work. Sprained tendons will never be prevented by the application of ordinary bandages or boots, for example, but by avoiding the over-flexion of the joint, which is their main cause, and this relates directly to the type of work the horse does and the ground conditions he is subjected to.

On the brighter side, judging by the scientific reports on them, a new addition to the equestrian market, called **Professional's Choice Sports Medicine Boots**, really do seem to lessen stress and give significant support to the lower leg. Normally, the only way actually to support a leg is to apply some type of cast or bandage in such a way as to prevent the

'Professional's Choice Sports Medicine Boots' which claim to give protection from knocks, absorb concussion and give support without interfering with the action of the fetlock joint.

fetlock joint moving too much, thus reducing the movement of, and stress on, tendons and ligaments. With Sports Medicine Boots, about a quarter of the stress-causing energy, usually absorbed by the leg during work, is absorbed by the boots instead, lessening the load the legs have to bear and so reducing the likelihood of injury. These boots would be well worth investigating by any owner of an athletic horse.

Also on the market are various makes of boots, bandages and leg wraps that claim to retain warmth and so help to promote blood circulation and healing in an injured leg. After roughly the first 48 hours following injury, by which time it is hoped that treatment and rest will have reduced the heat and swelling, the aim is to keep the circulation going and these rehabilitation products do seem to help in this.

BOOTS

There is a traditional range of boots aimed at protecting the legs from knocks rather than sprains. These boots are now made from various synthetic materials as well as the traditional boxcloth, felt and leather. Various shock-absorbing synthetics seem ideal for boots and they also have easy-care qualities which make them attractive to busy owners and grooms. Woollen and leather materials take time to clean, launder and dry off, but synthetics normally shrug off water and can be just rinsed off in water and ready again in no time.

Brushing boots
Brushing boots are probably the most common leg protection used, along with their slightly longer counterparts, **speedicut boots**. A horse is said to brush in action when he kicks

his opposite leg low down on the fetlock and leg, whereas he is said to speedicut when he knocks himself higher up the leg, just below the knee or hock. With any leg boots, the foreboots are a little shorter and may have fewer straps than the hind boots as the horse's hind cannons are longer than the fore.

Brushing boots have hardened pads of leather or a synthetic material covering the inside of the fetlock joint and part of the way up the inside of the leg. They fasten with straps and buckles or clips, leather, Velcro or otherwise, on the outside of the leg (so that the horse does not kick the fastening undone) and with the ends of the straps (or whatever) pointing backwards so that they are not easily pulled undone should the horse go through undergrowth where twigs and branches might catch on the boots. Speedicut boots are made in the same way.

Tendon boots
Contrary to popular opinion, tendon boots are not intended to support the tendon (or, if they are, they don't) but to protect the tendons of the forelegs from being cut into by the hind hooves. They have firm padding down the back which fits down the back of the forelegs, with padded, reinforced, slightly flexible bars inside the boot which go up the grooves on the sides of the leg behind the cannons to help to stabilize the boot and stop it slipping round on the leg. Tendon boots fasten in the same way as brushing boots. Obviously, they are not intended for hind legs.

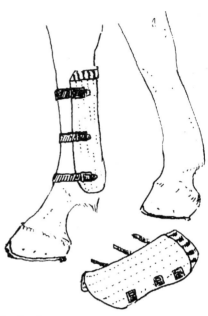

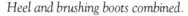

Heel and brushing boots combined.

Tendon boots.

Heel boots

Heel boots do not actually protect the horse's heel, which is part of his foot, but the underneath, ergot area of his fetlock. During hard or fast work, particularly when landing from a jump at speed, the force is such as to press the bottom of the fetlock right down onto the ground, and heel boots protect this area which can otherwise become bruised and even bleed. They have firm padding around the ergot and lower area of the joint and are sometimes found in a form that combines heel protection with protection of other areas such as tendons and the insides of the legs.

Shin boots

Conversely, shin boots protect the fronts of the cannons and are intend-ed to be worn for jumping when the horse might bang his legs on fences. The padding down the front of the leg aims to lessen such knocks.

Polo boots

There are various designs of polo boots on the market, which give hefty protection from kicks (self-inflicted or otherwise), knocks from the ball or mallet, etc. during the considerable rough and tumble of a polo game. They provide padded protection from just below the knee and hock right down to the coronet in many cases, often with flaps of protective material over the heels which can be injured in polo. They often fasten by means of integral bandages or sometimes with straps.

Over-reach boots

Over-reach boots are commonly seen and aim to protect the heels of the horse's forefeet from being trodden on by his own hind feet. This is common in young horses who have yet to gain full control of their balance and way of going, and also in weak horses and those in poor condition (when they should not really be worked). The ordinary sort look just like upside-down rubber bells and can be quite a job to get on (see illustration below left). Newer sorts have flaps or 'petals' of tough synthetic material on a band going round the pastern. They simply strap round and clip or buckle in place, and also obviate the common problem of the older type of boot turning inside out up over the fetlock where it is quite useless and can even interfere with the horse's action and upset him.

Knee pads

Knee pads come in two sorts. They are hard shields that cover the front of the knee and are attached to a padded band that is fastened around the leg just above the knee. There is a further strap fastened very loosely below the knee just to keep the shield down without interfering with the horse's action. Their object is to protect the front of the knee should the horse fall, either when travelling or at exercise, but they are not secure enough for fast work or jumping.

The sort used for travelling have rugging material around the shield but the exercise type, often called skeleton knee pads, do not.

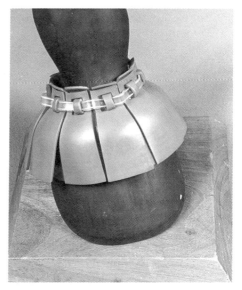

A conventional rubber over-reach boot. These are difficult to put on and remove and often turn upside down in use.

The improved-design 'petal'-type over-reach boots which are easier to put on (strapping round the pastern) and which do not turn upside down on the leg.

Hock boots

Hock boots are meant solely for travelling and consist of padded cups of leather or some synthetic material surrounded by rugging or another fabric, which fit over the points of the hocks and strap on like knee pads – firmly at the top and looser below. They aim to protect the point of the hock from knocks during travelling and are sometimes used on horses in the stable if they have the habit of kicking the walls with their hind legs or scraping away bedding before lying down. Horses do not find them comfortable to wear all the time, however, and a better, if more expensive, measure is to use resilient flooring and wall protection.

Travelling boots

Travelling boots give almost full-leg protection, often extending from above the knee or hock right down to the coronet and heel. They are a quick, easy alternative to the traditional travelling wear of stable/travelling bandages over padding, combined with separate knee pads, hock boots and over-reach boots in front to protect the horse should he tread on himself while trying to keep his balance while travelling. Travelling boots are usually made of synthetic materials and are very quick and easy to apply. They can fasten with tapes, straps and buckles, straps and clips or Velcro, as can other synthetic boots. They are light and 'easy care' while still giving good protection. Some horses find their 'feel' a little strange and should be gradually accustomed to wearing them regulary whilst in the stable.

Types of boots

U brushing – to protect the fetlocks against knocks, worn all round

U tendon – to protect the tendons on the back of the forelegs

U heel – to protect the ergot of the fetlock against bruises and cuts in fast work, worn all round

U shin – to protect the front of the cannon bones when jumping

U polo – to protect against blows, worn from the knee or hock to the coronet, sometimes with heel flaps also, worn all round

U over-reach – to protect against treading on front heels by hind feet, forefeet only

U knee pads – to protect against falls on the road during exercise or against knocks when travelling

U hock – to protect against knocks when travelling

U travelling – to protect against knocks and treads when travelling, worn from above the knee or hock down over the coronet and heel, worn all round

BANDAGES

There are basically two types of leg bandages: exercise or work bandages and stable/travelling bandages (the same thing).

Exercise bandages

The best and most useful sort of exercise bandage is made of a stretchy crêpe fabric which *must* be (but often is not) put on over leg padding such as gamgee as the fabric has a self-tightening effect on the leg and can really cut into the skin and underlying tissues if applied unevenly, just a little too tightly or with the tapes alone tied too tight. Severe cutting and bruising, with the associated swelling and even splitting open of a badly swollen leg, can easily take place with incorrectly applied exercise bandages and their application is a job for the knowledgeable. Of course, everyone has to learn, but it would be well worth a novice's while to pay a professional for a proper lesson on how to apply bandages (perhaps instead of a riding lesson some time) and to practise on table legs at home before letting themselves loose on a horse. All you need is instruction, common sense and, as ever, a realization that horses are flesh and blood and prone to injury.

The illustrations below show how to apply exercise bandages. Basically, the points to watch are that the padding (whatever sort you choose) must come just above and below the bandage to prevent the top and bottom cutting into the leg, it must be smooth and the bandage must be applied with an even, snug, but not tight, tension all the way down. Just as important, the tapes must be fastened at the same tension. If everything is too loose it will all unravel and trip the horse; if too tight it will do the damage already described above.

Bandage tapes can be plain, sewn-on tapes, have Velcro fastenings or thread through metal Ds sewn onto

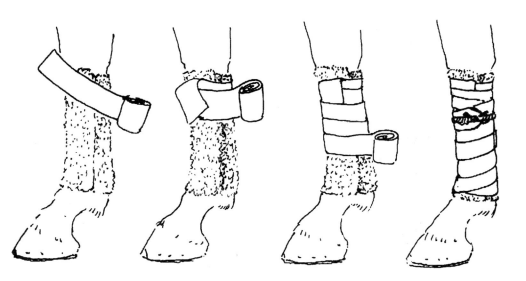

To put on an exercise bandage first place the padding smoothly round the leg with a double thickness over the tendons at the back. Position the bandage as shown and take a full turn round the leg. Then let the spare end fall down and bandage over it to help secure the end. (Bandage over it higher than shown here; the drawing is only for explanation.) Finish by tying the tapes no tighter than the bandage itself on the outside of the leg. Some people like to take the padding and bandage partly under the fetlock at the back to give more protection here.

reinforced sections of bandage.
A very secure way of fastening
bandages is to sew them on. Masking
and other adhesive tape can also be
applied over the fastening as a
worthwhile belt-and-braces
operation.

Stable or travelling bandages

Stable or travelling bandages are
wider and should be longer than
exercise bandages and the most
useful and easy type to apply are
made of knitted woollen material.

You can get rather expensive
deluxe velour ones but these are
stiffer, more difficult to put on, not so
warm in my view and do not mould
to the leg as well as the cheaper sort.
Tapes and fastenings are as for exercise bandages. Many people feel that

*A stable bandage is applied as an exercise
bandage but goes right down to the coronet
band at the top of the hoof. To remove
both types of bandage, undo the tapes and
quickly pass the fabric from hand to hand
around the leg without rolling it. Then rub
the leg briskly to stimulate circulation in
the skin.*

stable bandages are too short these
days and some may sew two sets
together to get one useful, super-
length set of bandages. Although
more expensive initially, it is well
worth it to have the extra length.

These bandages are applied from

Padding materials

Both work and stable bandages must
be put on over padding, although you
may see the latter without this and not
infrequently even the former, too.

The type of padding you use is
important. The worst and most useless
is sheets of plastic foam padding. This
compresses to nothing under the
crêpe. However, if anyone also tells
you that it also makes horses' legs
sweat, take no notice – horses' legs
don't sweat.

Gamgee tissue (cotton wool inside a
gauze mesh covering) is still very
widely used for padding and is
very good if fresh and resilient but,
particularly if it gets wet, it soon loses
that resilience and has to be replaced
frequently, an on-going expense
avoided by buying longer-lasting
branded paddings that can be washed
and reused. Such paddings are
resilient and do their job well. Cotton
wool alone can be used but tends to
disintegrate without the gauze
covering of Gamgee.

For stable/travelling bandages, you
can use the same paddings but as
these bandages are also used to help
dry off wet legs, you will also find
squares of mesh woollen or cotton bed
blanketing or anti-sweat rug fabric
useful. These trap air beneath the
bandage and really help dry off the
legs. Cotton knitted dishcloths do the
same job.

just below the knee or hock to right over the fetlock and covering the pastern, the aim being warmth and protection at the same time. The same rules apply for tension and evenness, although, due to the fabric being softer, you are not quite so likely to make errors with stable bandages. However, it should be said that it is common to see wavy lines on legs indicating the uneven pressure of badly applied bandages. If an injury is caused, white rings may even develop round the legs once it has healed if the hair follicles have been damaged.

Tail bandages

This is one type of bandage under which padding is not normally used, mainly, I feel, because it is tricky to apply it. However, the underneath of a horse's tail is only skin and tails are regularly injured when tight tail bandages are unevenly applied. In severe cases it has been known for the circulation to get cut off to such an extent that the tail has 'died' and dropped off! I am not exaggerating.

When applying any bandage, including tail bandages, it is useful to damp the hair to give a bit of extra grip, but do not damp the material itself, as this may then shrink as it dries and become too tight. (Presumably this should also happen if horses get their legs wet when wearing exercise bandages during work but nobody seems to bother about this, maybe because these bandages are removed as soon as the horse finishes work and before the fabric has a chance to dry out and shrink.) Tail bandages should not be left on all night nor all the time during very long journeys.

Tail bandages are used to fine down and smooth the top of the tail after grooming and to protect it against rubs (maybe under a tail guard) during travelling. They are normally made of the same crêpe fabric as exercise bandages and often an exercise bandage is used. Knitted cotton stockinette, occasionally used for exercise bandages, can also be used for tails and docs not have the same, potentially dangerous, self-tightening effect, so it is safer.

CHAPTER 9

CLOTHING

Many people are surprised to learn that you can do considerable harm to a horse by providing him with unsuitable and, particularly, badly fitting clothing. The horse wears his rug and maybe also under-rugs or blankets, for many hours a day, whether he is indoors or turned out, and a strongly made rug digging in and rubbing in all the wrong places for 22 hours can cause significant sores not to mention distress to the horse.

Unfortunately, lots of rugs *look* as though they fit and owners may leave them on quite happily, but a close check of the horse's demeanour and, even more revealing, of his body and coat may show that the rug is, in practice, rubbing and causing him irritation and possibly even pain. It is not only the fit of the individual rug to the particular horse that matters but also the design. Horses are not flat with straight backs, like so many rugs! Horse-shaped rugs are as important as well-designed and fitted tack.

TYPES OF RUG

There are still four basic types of rug on the market but with lots of variations on these four themes. There are day rugs, night rugs, stable rugs and New Zealand or turnout rugs. In addition there are lightweight summer sheets (rugs of cotton or linen) and work clothing called exercise sheets, quarter sheets or work sheets, which are like ordinary rugs although lighter in weight and without the front fastening. There are also various therapeutic rugs which claim to help in the healing of injuries, such as torn muscles and other soft-tissue injuries, by promoting blood circulation, and at least one brand filled with polystyrene beads which claims to help to heal injuries and to be particularly good in cases of arthritis by creating an opposite electrical charge to that given out naturally by the body, and which does, in practice, seem to help.

Day rugs
Day rugs are meant for day wear when the horse will probably not be lying down a great deal and, in any case, his bed will be, or should be, receiving regular attention in the way of skepping out droppings. The rug should not, therefore, be subjected to manure stains which can be difficult to remove, and can be made of luxurious woollen material bound in contrasting or toning fabric and bearing the owner's initials,

family crest, company logo or whatever. I think a nice touch is to put the horse's name on his rug. Such rugs do look lovely and still find a ready market.

Night rugs

Night rugs, on the other hand, are made of much rougher, cheaper material, such as jute or canvas, with a similar binding and, as such fabrics are not warm, may be unlined, half-lined or fully lined in grey woollen material or, for better quality, checked woollen material. The horse frequently lies down during the night and also rolls and, obviously, cannot very well avoid his own droppings, so the rug becomes stained, hence the rougher, cheaper fabric.

Stable rugs

Stable rugs are modern synthetic-fabric rugs designed to take all or most of the hassle out of laundering heavy, dirty horse rugs and, because they are so (comparatively) easily laundered, can be used day and night, hence the lack of differentiation between day and night garments. Many of them are also warmer than traditional fabrics particularly when compared with the weight of the latter, and it is here that synthetics really score. The horse is relieved of the weight of a rug plus perhaps two, three or more woollen blankets beneath to provide adequate warmth in winter when most of his coat may have been clipped off to enable him to work without sweating excessively and, therefore losing condition. Synthetic rugs may have separate liners which clip in.

Blankets

Blankets to go under traditional or modern rugs are of wool, the best being called Witney blankets, made of thick golden-coloured wool with red and black stripes – good enough to use on your own bed or in the car! Others may be of grey, brown or fawn wool and are lighter and thinner and there is something to be said for the argument that two thinner blankets are warmer than one thick one. You can also get synthetic blankets, usually made of acrylic, which are cheaper and easier to wash but less warm.

Because modern synthetic rugs normally fasten more loosely than traditional ones and have different fastenings, ordinary blankets do not usually stay in place under them. To combat this, manufacturers have brought out various synthetic under-rugs which clip to their top rugs with studs or other fastenings or Velcro. However, many due to their good shape and fit, stay in place under a top rug on their own, simply fastening at the breast. Feel your horse's ears and flanks to check if he is cold and needs extra clothing.

FASTENINGS

Traditional rugs invariably fasten with a strap at the breast and a roller or stitched-on surcingle round the girth/ribcage. The breast strap is all right and unavoidable, but the roller/surcingle arrangement is anti-quated and very uncomfortable for the horse no matter how carefully you try to adjust it.

Of the two, the padded, separate roller is by far the best. The roller, of leather or fabric, is wide and has pads that sit on either side of the horse's spine: there is a space between them which aims to leave the spine clear of pressure, although the poorer designs and makes do not have enough space here. In a good design, this also 'wedges' the roller in place and stops it sliding or twisting around. However, the rug and blankets beneath it do still slip about in practice, usually down the sides and, in the case of blankets, backwards over the tail.

If a separate, unpadded surcingle, is used the horse does not even have the comfort and slight security of the back padding. The surcingle will press relentlessly on the spine and does almost nothing to keep the rug and blankets in place. Most people place a thick pad of blanketing or foam under the surcingle on the spine, but this does little to resolve the problems.

In addition to the roller, some horses are additionally encumbered with a canvas or webbing breastgirth fastened to the roller to stop it slipping back when the owner or groom tries to give the horse a little more comfort by not fastening the roller too tightly!

Modern rugs fasten in a different and far better way altogether. They normally have some sort of thin surcingles which criss-cross under the horse's belly. They are stitched to the top half of the rug, at the front and back of the rug, and are loose on the lower parts, sometimes being completely detachable here, passing diagonally from right to left and front to back. For instance, the surcingle on the left front of the rug passes under the belly and clips to its partner on the right back part of the rug, and those on the opposite sides do the same.

Because modern rugs are horse-shaped, they have the advantage not only of being comfortable but of staying in place and righting themselves as the horse moves. The surcingles, therefore, simply keep the rug from actually falling off, although the opposing pull on the diagonally fastened surcingles does help somewhat with the self-righting effect.

Some makes have slightly different arrangements, perhaps with straps coming from the breast, passing down between the forelegs and coming up to fasten on the side or hip at each side, with, perhaps, other surcingles linking through from the shoulder or elsewhere, forming under-belly harnesses. This sounds complicated but is not in practice, and they all seem to work well. They increase the horse's comfort, in combination with good shaping, because they are not fastened at all tightly. This is their whole point. You must be able to get the width of your hand between the surcingle and the horse or rug for a comfortable but effective adjustment.

On traditional day rugs (and exercise clothing) there is a braided string called a fillet string that passes behind the horse's thighs above the point of his hocks, to stop the rug blowing up over his back and scaring him into a panic. On modern synthetic stable rugs, there is often a fillet strap or string combined with front-end surcingles to help to keep the rug on.

SHAPING

Good shaping is fundamental to a good rug and the horse's comfort and, therefore, good horse management. A good rug, when seen from the side when *off* the horse, should have a rise for the withers, dip slightly for the back, rise again for the croup and dip again towards the root of the tail, so following the shape of the horse's back like a good tailored jacket made for a human. In addition, there should be (but still often is not) darting or tucks round the neckline and back edge and/or at least darting behind the elbow and in front of the stifle, to shape the rug here and allow room for the hips and, particularly, the points of the shoulders which almost always come in for significant rubbing and pressure from clothing.

Just because a rug has all these shaping features does not mean, of course, that it will actually fit your horse, so you should try a few to check that the shaping accords with his individual body.

RUGS FOR OUTDOORS

Paddock rugs or **sheets** are intended for throwing over a horse in the collecting ring at a show or for leading the horse round the paddock at a race meeting. They are very like lightweight day rugs but some come in showerproof or actually waterproof materials, when they are often called rain sheets. They are not substantial and are not intended for use when turning the horse out into his field. They are also not intended for use in the stable.

Fitting rugs
Design and shaping are not the same as fit and size. You measure a rug from the front of the breast right back to the back edge and will find that they are measured in centimetres or 3in increments.

A rug of any sort must come in *front* of the withers, not, as so very many do, rest on top of them where it will be pulled down and back by the horse's own movements and its own weight. This can cause rubbed hair or sore and even badly swollen withers which can put the horse off work.

At the back, the rug must come right back as far as the root of the tail, not finish half-way up his quarters or even at his croup as so many do: it will not keep the horse warm if it finishes short.

In depth, the rug should come just below the level of the horse's elbow and stifle.

New Zealand or turnout rugs must have the same elements of good fit but can be a little roomier, and should extend a little past the root of the tail.

Turnout rugs
For this, you need a New Zealand, Australian or turnout rug. Most such rugs are referred to as New Zealand rugs because the excellent design they all follow (or the best do, anyway) originated in New Zealand where they keep their horses out much more than we do in the UK because of the kinder climate, at least in the North Island. The original New Zealand rug is sold in the UK as the Emston, which has all the good points of shaping and the essential, self-righting quality. The Emston and similar rugs fasten at the

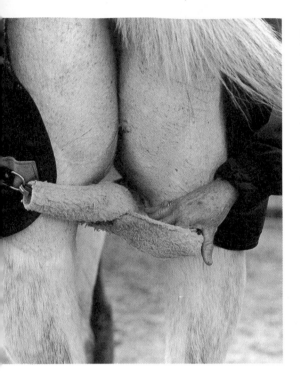

New Zealand rug leg straps. Linking them through each other like this is generally the best way to fasten them. These straps have sheepskin sleeves to prevent them rubbing the sensitive skin inside the hind legs. The hand's width between the strap and the horse is the correct fit, although with the added bulk caused by the sleeves, perhaps these straps could do with being a hole or two looser, but no more.

breast and have hind leg straps that fasten to the sides of the rug and either cross over between the hind legs so that the left strap fastens on the right back edge of the rug and vice versa or, far better in my experience, link through each other, as illustrated above. This method seems to help to keep the back of the rug in place and also holds the straps away

from the sensitive skin between the horse's hind legs and helps to prevent rubbing here, although you can buy sheepskin or synthetic fleece sleeves for this (which obviously have to be kept clean). Some people use bicycle-tyre inner tubes to cover the straps.

Australian-type rugs have front, as opposed to hind, leg straps which clip on at the breast and pass down between the forelegs then up to fasten one on each side of the rug in front of the hip or stifle. There is also a fillet strap to help to stabilize the back of the rug. My experience is that this design, despite its good shaping features, does not stay in place as well as the hind-leg fastening type.

Other outdoor rugs that have similar features, variations of the same leg straps (hind or fore) and underbelly surcingles or harnesses are justifiably popular and, as they are made of lightweight synthetic fabrics which mostly shrug off water, are *much* lighter in wear than the canvas of the traditional rugs.

Modern turnout rugs may have additional clip-in linings for extra warmth, whereas the traditional ones have half linings of wool. Do not buy a full woollen lining as the bottom edge will get wet and damp will creep up inside the rug.

There have been problems with leaking in modern synthetic turnout rugs but ever enterprising manufacturers are now overcoming these problems. The line of stitching down the spine is the main problem as the rugs tend to leak here through the stitching holes. This problem now seems to be being solved with special thread that expands to fill the holes tightly when wet.

These rugs also sometimes use special 'rip-stop' fabrics for their outer coverings and can be very tough and hard-wearing in use, justifying their high price. The ultimate would be a rug that allowed natural body moisture to evaporate up through the lining and fabric while at the same time stopping rainwater getting in. Although the fabrics may permit this in practice when clean, no one has yet overcome the problem of the rug becoming plastered with wet mud when the horse rolls, which effectively stops the 'breathable' effect. However, these rugs do not develop problems of clamminess inside them

so perhaps this idealistic aim is not really necessary.

As horses that have been turned out inevitably spend a lot of time with their heads down, rooting for whatever grass they can find, even on a mud patch, it is essential that the front end fits comfortably. Any rug, indoor or out, should fit snugly round the base of the neck like a collar (not press down on the shoulder blades) but should have the breast straps low enough to permit the horse to get his head down and graze or root in his bedding if he wants – this is particularly important in a turnout rug. Pressure on the breast strap will pull the rug down on the withers and cause pressure here, which is precisely what we

Textiles for rugs

Traditional winter clothing is made of natural fabrics – wool, jute, canvas. Lightweight summer clothing, intended for use on groomed, stabled horses and ponies in warm weather, to protect against dust and flies, has traditionally been made of cotton and linen (this sort of clothing being called summer sheets).

Synthetic textiles used in the manufacture of horse clothing are many and varied. They nearly all have the advantage of being easier and quicker to wash and dry than traditional fabrics, a great plus point, and of being lighter in wear and, normally, more hardwearing as well.

The most recent development is that they are often 'breathable' or permeable, which means they allow the sweat produced by the horse to evaporate up through the fabric, so maintaining a

comfortable, healthy 'body atmosphere'. Traditional fabrics also do this, but early synthetic clothing was made of nylon which hindered this evaporation. Nylon is still used for some clothing, usually combined with polyester quilting, and this works well in practice. Some permeable fabrics are showerproof and some actually claim to be waterproof.

In addition, fleecy (usually acrylic) under-rugs and linings are available for modern rugs, while woollen blankets can be used under traditional clothing.

Heat-retaining fabrics are now quite widely used for extra warmth in winter and for helping to heal various injuries and soothe the symptoms of arthritis. It is important never to use them in a box containing a heat lamp as the extra heat generated and retained by the rug can actually burn the horse underneath his rug.

wish to avoid. If the neckline is too tight and the breast strap too high, an uncomfortable stricture is created by the strap pressing against the horse's gullet at the base of his neck, so check this on your horse when he has his head down. You should be able to pass the flat of your hand comfortably all round the neckline for correct fit.

Types of rugs

∪ day – very smart woollen rugs with contrasting binding

∪ night – jute or canvas, lined with wool

∪ stable – synthetic fabrics, light and warm

∪ blankets – wool or synthetics, worn under night rugs

∪ turnout – canvas or synthetic, lined with wool, or synthetic fabric

∪ summer sheets – cotton or linen, with fillet string

∪ exercise sheets – wool mostly but waterproof ones also available, with fillet string

∪ rain sheets – waterproof, usually nylon, with fillet string

∪ therapeutic – claim to help in the healing of injuries to muscles and soft tissues

∪ anti-sweat – cotton 'string vest' style to help evaporation of sweat and the drying of horses

Anti-sweat rugs

These are not new but still have a valuable place in the horse's wardrobe. They are simply string vests for horses and they work on the principle of trapping an extra layer of air next to the horse's skin to assist with drying off. They do not actually stop the horse sweating but make it possible for the sweat to evaporate under a top rug of any material. They can also be used in place of a blanket for extra warmth without weight, because of the body-warmed air they hold next to the horse.

They are often seen used alone which was not their originally intended use. When used this way they do, in fact, cool and dry off a hot horse faster than if they were used under a top rug, because the uneven texture of the mesh creates little currents of air over the surface of the horse, which has the same effect as lots of tiny cooling breezes. Because of this, they are actually too cold to wear alone on a cold day and should therefore not be used alone in cold weather as the horse may cool down too rapidly and become chilled. A top rug should also be put on on these occasions.

EXERCISE CLOTHING

Exercise clothing is most widely used in racing circles. The idea is that if a horse is fully clipped and suddenly brought out to work on a cold day (most racehorses being thin-skinned Thoroughbreds) he will be too cold and clammed up to work properly, will not be mentally willing and, if worked while cold, he could suffer muscle damage as muscles need to be warmed up and 'worked in' gently before being asked for strenuous effort.

Exercise sheets are usually made of lightweight wool, but waterproof fabrics are also used and some modern designs are made so that they fit round the saddle and can be put on quickly and easily without having to remove the saddle. Normally, a traditional sheet is placed on the horse's back first and then the saddle is put on on top of it. There are usually loops running along the bottom edge, where the binding is, for the girth to be run through, anchoring the sheet in place. It is essential that a fillet string be used.

HOODS

Head and neck hoods are available for turnout and work and also for travelling. They can be used for extra warmth and to help to keep the horse clean. Traditional and synthetic fabrics are both available. Traditional woollen ones usually match the day rug and fasten loosely with tapes below the neck. Those meant for turning out strap, tie or clip to special hooks on their accompanying turnout rug. There are also close-fitting, stretchy ones that can be used to keep the mane flat (poor horse!) or for protecting against mud in the field.

Horses are amazingly tolerant creatures, but I cannot help feeling that many people over-burden them quite unnecessarily with clothing of all sorts. I find it particularly upsetting to see native ponies turned out in warm, even hot, weather wearing New Zealand rugs because their small and obviously unknowledgeable owners feel that this will keep the pony clean or protect (quite unnecessarily) against a sudden shower! They obviously have no conception of how very uncomfortable and distressed the pony must feel.

In its place, clothing of all sorts is useful and beneficial, but like so much else in the horse world, it can easily be misused. It should always be used with discretion, judgement and knowledge, when it will fulfill its purposes of protecting the horse and making him more comfortable, rather than upsetting or even positively torturing him.

CHAPTER 10

CARE AND MAINTENANCE

As you will find out when you come to equip your horse, good tack and clothing are expensive, but as time goes by you will also find that they can last many years, several horses' lifetimes in fact, if well cared for, depending on the individual item. Even textiles can last for many years, given good care, unless your horse is particularly rough on them.

The keys to long life as far as tack and clothing are concerned are regular cleaning and care and the attentions of a good saddler when necessary.

LEATHER

Leather is not difficult to care for but it can be time consuming and rather labour intensive! Basically, all leather needs the same care – washing clean of sweat, grease and mud, soaping with a good, preferably glycerine-based, saddle soap, periodic dressing with a suitable leather conditioner if it is not used very often or if it gets very wet, and storage in a fairly warm, fairly dry atmosphere, flat or on supportive racks. Care in use, such as avoiding scratching the leather or general abuse, goes without saying, but this does not mean

your leather items have to be mollycoddled. They will stand up to hard wear if in good condition.

Cleaning leather

To clean leather, first assemble your equipment – a bucket of lukewarm water (you cannot remove grease with cold water) with perhaps just a dash of a very mild washing up liquid in it if the tack is very greasy, saddle soap, washing sponge, soaping sponge, perhaps a chamois leather or substitute for drying off the leather a bit and maybe metal polish if you are intending to clean buckles and other items (not normally done every time the tack is cleaned).

I find it easier to take everything to pieces, including bridles, rather than move buckles up or down a hole and fiddle with keepers and runners in an effort to keep the bridle together, but not everyone agrees. You do have to strip your saddle (take off the girth and stirrup leathers) to do it properly, but here again this is not strictly necessary if you are in a hurry. It is very little trouble, though.

You can rest your saddle on a saddle horse, on the back of a chair or on your lap – anywhere will do provided it does not damage the saddle and enables you to get at both the top and underside easily. If leaving it in one piece, you will find it easier to hang the bridle on a proper bridle-cleaning hook (see illustration opposite) suspended from the ceiling, or from hooks fixed to the wall; otherwise, you can take it to pieces (reassembling it in accordance with the illustration below) and work on a table or even on your lap if you have to.

A bridle hook is ideal for cleaning a bridle if you don't want to take it to pieces, and can also be used for stirrup leathers. It should be taken down after use as it is very easy to sustain a nasty head injury on it.

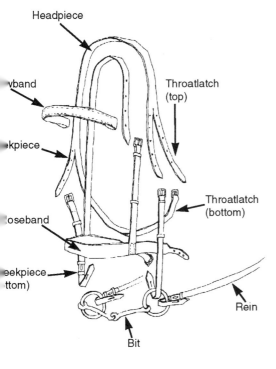

Headpiece

vband

kpiece

oseband

eekpiece
ttom)

Throatlatch
(top)

Throatlatch
(bottom)

Rein

Bit

Parts of a bridle ready to reassemble. Start by threading the throatlatch and tops of the cheekpieces (all in one with the headpiece) down through the browband loops. The noseband's headstall is then threaded through the loops under the headpiece, up through the left loop and down through the right one, then the bottom halves of the cheekpieces are buckled on and finally the bit and the reins are attached.

Very muddy tack should be rinsed off in water to remove the mud, as wiping it off with the sponge will rub the grains against the leather and scratch it. However, be very careful not to let water get into the stuffing under your saddle seat as this can spoil and harden it and make it lumpy and thinner, as well as taking a very long time to dry out properly.

With your washing sponge dipped in the warm water and wrung out, rub off all grease and dried sweat: there will obviously be most on the parts that actually touch the horse. Any little, hard, black blobs of grease (called 'jockeys') you may find must be gently scraped off with the edge of a coin or a *blunt* knife. All grease and dirt must be washed off carefully and thoroughly, as soaping over the top hardens it on, does not benefit the leather and can subsequently cause sores on the horse.

When the leather is clean, dry off the surplus moisture, if any, with the chamois and move on to the soaping. Your soaping sponge must never be actually wetted. Dip your bar of soap into clean water, or put a little water on the soap in your tin, whichever is appropriate, and rub the sponge on that. Then, using small, firm, circular movements, rub the soap thoroughly into all surfaces, nooks and crannies of the leather, paying particular attention to the flesh ('rough') side of the leather, where the leather touches the horse and also where it gets most wear, such as where it turns round metal (round bit rings, through the stirrup eye, over the stirrup bar, behind buckles, etc., which is why you must move buckles down a hole so that you can get at these parts).

The circular motion is fine for expanses of leather such as your saddle flaps and panels, but not for long strips like straps, stirrup leathers, reins and so on. For these, simply wrap the sponge round the leather and move it firmly up and down the strap.

The trick with soaping is not to have the sponge too wet: if it lathers, the sponge is far too wet and the soap is not, in fact, doing its job properly.

When you have finished soaping, your leather should have a smooth, deep sheen to it. Poke excess soap out of any holes with a matchstick or twig.

If dressing your leather with a conditioning leather dressing such as a branded product or neatsfoot oil, follow the directions carefully as too much oil can make your leather

Cleaning buckles
If you are cleaning buckles, do your best to make sure the metal polish does not get onto the leather, as it can rot it and, if it does, wash it off at once. *Never* put metal polish on the bit mouthpiece, only on the rings or cheeks, not near the mouth, and polish it off very thoroughly.

horribly slimy and can actually weaken it. If the leather is in regular use and is cleaned frequently (ideally after each outing, although few working owners can manage this), dressing is hardly ever necessary.

It is easier to clean stirrup leathers by hooking the buckle onto some convenient hook or the bridle cleaning hook and running your sponges up and down them. Put the right leather back on the left side of the saddle and vice versa, so that each receives equal stress when the rider mounts from the nearside, as is usual, otherwise they will stretch unevenly and cause you to ride unevenly unless you compensate by adjusting the leathers.

The breast and leg straps of rugs are cleaned in much the same way, as are all leather items, from boots to headcollars.

FABRIC ITEMS

If your girth is of fabric with only a little leather for the buckle attachments, scrub it clean with a nail-brush and mild soap, rinse it very thoroughly in clear water and hang it by the buckles at both ends in a

U-shape, so that water does not run down on to them, possibly rusting them.

Give fabric reins the same treatment, cleaning the leather with saddle soap afterwards.

Bandages can be a problem to wash until you discover that washing them inside an old pillowcase in the washing machine on a short programme does the job well and prevents them tangling up and being almost impossible, and extremely time consuming, to undo.

Woollen blankets must be washed in the same way as woollen clothing for humans. You can have them dry cleaned, and most day rugs usually are, but this does not get them really clean. If you wash *and rinse* them in cold to lukewarm water, using a mild, non-biological washing product and adding fabric softener to the last rinse (as you would bed blankets) you will have no problems. You can tumble dry them on warm or spin and dry them on a clothes airer. Even your best day rugs can be washed this way, but stick to cool to cold temperatures to avoid significant shrinkage. It is not necessary to remove leather parts first. Just give them a good dressing before and after washing.

Jute night rugs can be washed in a large machine or in a tub or old bath using washing soda. Proprietary washing powders *can* be used but even if you rinse really thoroughly some can remain and may cause skin reactions in some horses, particularly the modern biological powders. Jute and similar rugs are a problem if they have woollen linings, as if you wash them in hand-hot water to get out the muck stains you will shrink the

lining and pull the rug out of shape. The best thing to do is to use just slightly warm water with washing soda or a mild, non-biological washing product and put up with the stains.

Cotton or linen summer sheets or numnahs can be washed safely in hand-hot water (40-50°C) with a similar product, but be sure to wash synthetics strictly in accordance with the maker's instructions, as otherwise you can damage the item and its lining or filling, if any, making it subsequently useless. Most are simple to wash and you can spin them with impunity, tumble them on the correct temperature, hang them on a rack, drape them over the cistern or even over a hedge or fence and they will usually dry quickly and without problems.

Some rugs with thermal linings must be washed very carefully as regards temperature as hot temperatures in the washer or dryer can actually melt the filling into a hard, useless lump. If there is no laundry label on any rug you buy, get instructions from the saddler or manufacturer, preferably in writing, as if you wash it incorrectly and things go wrong, you will have no recompense and rugs can be expensive to replace.

Any fabric (usually synthetic) that is waterproof or showerproof will need reproofing, maybe every time it is laundered, so find out about this from the saddler or maker and don't be fobbed off by vague answers. You can get reproofing products from either source (or should be able to) and by following the instructions carefully you should not have any problems.

To clean a traditional canvas turnout rug, which will obviously not go into a washing machine successfully, if at all, hang it up by the rings on the back edge from strong hooks specially fitted into a wall somewhere on your premises, and hose and scrub off all mud from the outside. Lay it flat, lining up, on the ground and vacuum off all surplus dust, dirt and hair (get four friends to stand one on each corner of the lining to prevent it getting tangled up in the vacuum's rotary brush!), then gently scrub the lining with warm, soapy water. Then hang the rug up again and hose all the soap out really thoroughly with clear *warm* water – if you use cold water the lining may shrink; the trick in washing wool being to use water of the same cold to warm temperature for both washing and rinsing. (You can wash the lining in cold water, of course.) If the lining is detachable, wash it separately just like a woollen blanket.

Dry the rug by hanging it on a clothes rack or over a hedge or fence on a good day, turning it frequently. It will be far too heavy for a clothes line. Laundering a traditional turnout rug is quite a big job, so, as you can imagine, most people don't do it every week! In between times, just remove any mud and vacuum the lining regularly, clean and oil the leather parts and keep a little oil smeared on metal fittings.

Generally, cleaning any item is largely a matter of common sense. If in doubt, fabrics can be treated as you would treat a garment of your own that is made of the same material, while leather is easy once you know how, and now you do.

Storage

Common sense indicates that dry storage in a place that is neither very cold nor hot is best. Traditional fabrics may be subject to attack by insects but synthetics can also form super nests for insects and small mammals, so periodic inspection is advised. You can use moth balls and the like but they leave the clothing smelling terrible and the horses find this revolting, so it is best to avoid this method.

Textiles are best stored clean and folded flat in dry chests or drawers.

Leather, as mentioned earlier, should be stored at room temperature in a dryish atmosphere. Dress leather thoroughly before putting it away, having made sure all straps are straight and buckles smeared with a little oil. In the old days, leather was wrapped in oiled silk or wax paper before storage but few people do this these days. It is a good plan to store it on fabric, though, and to separate each layer with more fabric, such as old bed sheets, summer sheets, towels, stable rubbers or whatever is handy and clean. Plastic and polythene should not be used as they do not allow the free circulation of air.

Saddles can be stored on their racks if the atmosphere is suitable, with a fabric covering, maybe just an old bedsheet folded over them, to keep the dust off.

Whenever cleaning or handling your equipment, keep an automatic eye out for fraying or rotting stitching or fabric, especially girth tabs and stirrup leathers. Prompt repair will not only lengthen the life of your equipment but can save nasty accidents or even your life. A leg strap or surcingle coming off a rug can trip a horse and break his leg; a girth tab coming away could kill you.

INDEX

Page numbers in *italics* refer to an illustration